D0810722

Integrity and recovery

in

computer systems

The LSE/NCC monographs on Information Systems Analysis and Design

Over the long pioneering period in the development and teaching of systems analysis, in which the London School of Economics and the UK National Computing Centre have frequently co-operated, members of these two establishments have come to recognise the lack of suitable books for students of systems analysis and design. Much of the existing literature seemed inappropriate for one of several reasons. The majority of nearly relevant books belonged to some associated discipline such as Computer Science or Business Studies. Of the few books dealing centrally with systems analysis, most were of a general character and inevitably rather superficial. The few available studies in depth were more in the nature of research monographs.

A series of books was required that would be concerned with information systems in the broadest sense, that involved organisations of men and machines. Each text would cover some limited topic at a detailed level, whilst the complete series would explore and delineate the subject area. This series is intended to satifsy these needs with books that combine the thoroughness of good scholarship with the balanced judgement of the experienced practitioner. The practitioner as well as the student will find the texts valuable, for each will serve as a guide to a group of problems that are likely to be encountered in an assignment. Naturally some monographs will focus upon problems of using equipment, especially computers and communications devices, whilst others will focus upon the human aspects of using information. Despite their specialisation, the books will not just be texts in engineering, computing science, psychology or sociology but will treat the technical or human problems upon which they concentrate within the broader perspective of the information system as a whole. Indeed a proportion of the series will deal with selected aspects of whole systems or of the design process itself.

The editorial policy of the series is defined and controlled by an editorial board, two of whose members are also joint general editors of the series. The constitution of this editorial board is as follows:

R Boot	National Computing Centre
Prof A S Douglas	London School of Economics
A R B Griffiths	Partner, Duncan Bransom Ltd
J D Humphries (joint editor)	NCC Publications
Prof J R S Kistruck	University of Warwick
F Land	London School of Economics
Prof D Lefkovitz	University of Pennsylvania
P Livingstone	University of Manchester Institute of Science and Technology
G Penney	National Computing Centre
C Port	The Civil Service College
R K Stamper (joint editor)	London School of Economics
P F Sutherby	Tube Investments, STD Services Ltd
Dr S J Waters	London School of Economics

Information systems analysis and design series
series editors — R K Stamper and J D Humphries

Integrity
and
Recovery

in computer systems

by
Terry Gibbons MA MSc LBCS

published in conjunction
with
The London School of Economics
and Political Science

by

NCC PUBLICATIONS
Manchester, UK

HAYDEN BOOK COMPANY INC
Rochelle Park, New Jersey, USA

Keywords for information retrieval (drawn from the *NCC Thesaurus of Computing Terms*): Security of computer systems; fault-tolerant computing; reliability; error control

to the Bruces
who restored my sanity on Monday nights

First published in 1976 by
NCC Publications, The National Computing Centre Limited
Oxford Road, Manchester, M1 7ED, England
and
Hayden Book Company, Inc
50 Essex Street, Rochelle Park, New Jersey, 07662, USA

Distributed in the United States of America and in Canada by Hayden Book Company, Inc and in Europe by NCC Publications.

ISBN in USA **0 8104 5959 8**
ISBN in Europe **0 85012 130 2**
Library of Congress Catalog Card Number **75–39937**

Text set in 10/11 point Times through the NCC CAPRICORN computer-aided publishing system in England, and printed and bound in the United States of America.

PRINTING	1	2	3	4	5	6	7	8	9
YEAR	76	77	78	79	80	81	82	83	84

Contents

Acknowledgements

This book has been through several years of gestation, taking form first as a Master's thesis for the University of London. During this time I have discussed its subject with many people, and if they now see their thoughts appear here unacknowledged, I apologise for what I hope is my unconscious plagiarism.

My colleagues at Barclays Bank made a particularly valuable contribution. I should mention Stan Gray, Beck Haywood (now with Burroughs), Will Litchfield and Ivan Stevenson, whose ideas, experience, criticism and expertise were indispensable. I owe thanks, too, to the staff of Birkbeck College for their help and encouragement in the preparation of the original thesis, particularly Jim Inglis, my supervisor; also to Steve Marsh, who pursued a thesis on a parallel subject at Birkbeck.

In the preparation of the book itself, I had the help of many individuals and organisations, including:

Computer Analysts and Programmers; "Computing" journal; ICL Dataskil; Management Systems and Programming; Olav Marjasoo (Paisley College of Technology); P M Melliar-Smith (University of Newcastle); John Pritchard (National Computing Centre); Peter Sebborn (Arthur Guiness and Son); Smiths Industries; Univac;

and I extend my thanks to all of them.

Finally I must acknowledge the help of Ronald Stamper, of the London School of Economics, whose advice and pointed criticism saved me from a number of literary disasters. If there are others which I have not succeeded in avoiding, I alone am responsible.

T K Gibbons
January 1976

Chapter 1

Introduction

This is a book for pessimistic systems designers. Pessimism is a valuable quality in a systems designer, and he should cultivate it with care, in defence against such persistent delusions as these:

- it is possible, with sufficient skill, care and patience, to build computer programs which are free of errors;
- systems break down only infrequently, therefore restart and recovery procedures are of only minor importance.

Such is the emotional attachment of people to their own brain-children that they can sustain these views in the face of regular and painful proofs to the contrary. The attitude adopted here is that computer systems do break down, often, at awkward times, in novel ways, and with what sometimes seems to be deliberate malice.

Consequently, the designer must think about recovery procedures from the very beginning of a system's life and at all stages thereafter. One cannot design an optimistic computer system and then tack on reliability and integrity as additional extras. These qualities are the product of positive and systematic pessimism and suspicion from the conception of the system through to live operation and maintenance. Should one ever be tempted to relax one's vigilance, one need only ponder on the forces arrayed against the computer system. Given reliable hardware, good design, conscientious programming and thorough testing, one may achieve a system which breaks down only infrequently. This means that the operators will be unfamiliar with the recovery procedures so that when they are required, as they inevitably will be, it can be virtually guaranteed that somebody will mount the wrong tape or press the wrong button. Of all the forces with which the designer has to contend, human frailty is the strongest.

In the cautious state of mind recommended for a systems designer, he constantly asks himself: "What can go wrong with this system? What can be done to prevent it, and what happens if it does go wrong?" This does not apply only to the computer system. The computer receives input from, delivers output to and operates in the context of larger systems: information systems, company or organisational systems, and even social systems. These systems can go wrong as well; in this book, which is mostly concerned with computer hardware, programs and data files, that is not usually our business, but the designer needs to know about these systems in so far as they make demands on the computer system design. Indeed, the correct operation of the computer can only be judged in the light of what the organisation it works for requires of it.

In broad terms, we judge the correct operation of an information-processing system by these standards:

–   it delivers correct output at the required time;
–   it does not accidentally lose any of the data it receives and stores, nor does it allow errors to be introduced;
–   it does not allow data to be read or modified except by those people authorised to do so.

Ensuring that a system meets these standards defines the subject of *security*. The system may fail to operate correctly as a result of an accident or failure in its environment, deliberate and malicious attack, or an internal failure in one of its own components. A secure system has to take account of all of these factors; thus, security is usually discussed under three headings: physical security, data security or privacy, and operational reliability.

Our interest is in the last. The term *operational reliability* can be used to describe the whole field of preventing and coping with internal faults in a computer system, including the people who are directly concerned with it. Computers do not require any external assistance to fail, either from human malefactors or from nature. Hardware faults, design mistakes, program bugs, and operational mixups provide plenty of opportunity for failure, and a wide scope for discussion. By *reliability*, we mean ensuring that the computer system operates normally, producing correct and timely output, and within this we include the subjects of *integrity* and *recovery*. Integrity covers the prevention, detection, confinement and correction of errors within the system. Recovery means repairing the system and restoring normal service after a failure.

That, then, is the ground covered by this book. It is difficult to draw the boundary exactly between operational reliability and the other aspects of computer security. For those readers who are interested in physical security and data privacy, the excellent, encyclopaedic book by James Martin (1) is recommended. Reference 7 is a useful survey of the field, and the EDP Analyzer reports (2 and 3) are a good introduction to the study of physical security. For those who are interested in security and privacy features in systems software, Popek (4) and Conway (5) are recommended, the former article having a vast bibliography. Finally, the EDP Analyzer report on computer fraud and embezzlement (6) is an interesting study of crime associated with computers in the United States.

References

1. James Martin, *Security, Accuracy and Privacy in Computer Systems*, Prentice-Hall, 1973.
2. *Security of the Computer Centre*, EDP Analyzer, vol 9, no 12, December 1971.
3. *Computer Security: Backup and Recovery Methods*, EDP Analyzer, vol 10 no 1, January 1972.
4. Gerald J Popek, *Protection Structures*, Computer, June 1974.
5. R W Conway, W L Maxwell, H L Morgan, *On the Implementation of Security Measures in Information Systems*, Communications of the ACM, vol 15, no 4, April 1972.
6. *Computer Fraud and Embezzlement*, EDP Analyzer, vol 11, no 9, September 1973.
7. *Where Next for Computer Security?*, NCC Publications 1974.

Chapter 2

Reliability, integrity and recovery: the scope of the problem

2.1 Concepts of recovery

In this book, we are concerned with a relatively limited class of systems. They are all designed and built for some specific purpose; they accept inputs and transform them in a useful way into outputs. Given the purpose of the system, we can ask such questions as: "How reliable is it?" or "Has it broken down?" We want to know how well it is doing the job for which it was designed, and this requires that somebody or something look at the outputs that the system produces and compare them with expected standards of behaviour.

This brings us to the idea of an *object system* and a *metasystem*. The object system is the one which is being examined. The metasystem is a larger system which includes it, provides it with its inputs and receives its outputs, and has some way of deciding whether or not it is working properly. The metasystem has a set of *criteria for acceptable operation* which it applies to the outputs from the object system, relative to the inputs given to it. If the criteria are not satisfied then, on the face of it, the object system is faulty. However, it is only designed to operate on specified types and ranges of inputs. If it is given something outside these specifications, it may fail through no fault of its own.

Inputs are usually validated by the object system before it accepts them, to make sure that they can be processed successfully. If they are invalid they are rejected, and the responsibility for deciding what to do about them is passed back to the metasystem. Even so, validation is only the application of fixed rules to detect certain anticipated types of error. An unexpected error may slip through the net and cause a failure anyway.

5

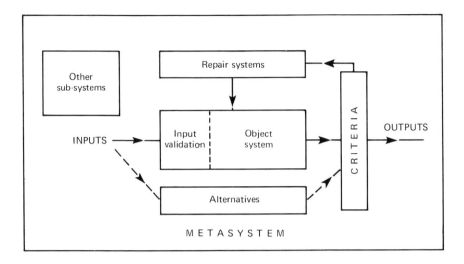

2.1   Object system and metasystem

Thus, if the object system fails, it may itself be faulty, or the fault may be in the metasystem or even in a still larger system which contains both of them. Whenever possible, the metasystem tries to find the location and nature of the fault and to work out a method of recovery. If it does not succeed, it has to pass the responsibility to a higher level still.

Recovery is the process of repairing the faulty system or component, putting right any damage it may have caused, and restoring it to normal operation. The errors introduced by the fault can be corrected in two ways. First, the metasystem can try to undo the damage by throwing away the work done by the faulty system and starting again. Secondly, it can apply corrections to compensate for the errors.

A simple example will illustrate the two methods. A computer-based accounting system fails in the middle of producing a batch of invoices. The simplest way to recover may be to throw away some or all of the invoices printed so far, repair the system, and start again. Suppose, on the other hand, that a minor, temporary fault were to cause a mistake in a single customer's invoice. To print the entire batch again would be wasteful; it is easier and cheaper to issue a correction for the single customer, even if this has to be done by hand.

Standards of acceptable operation and recovery procedures may be defined at several different levels within a system. Application programs may, for example, be able to handle limited types of errors in input data and some kinds of hardware fault. In the face of more serious faults, they either fail completely or are obliged to pass control back to their supervisory programs, which have wider recovery powers and may be able to correct the faults or find ways round them. Major hardware failures cannot be dealt with by the software at all: the entire processing system has to be halted, and recovery procedures may be invoked which involve operators, engineers, special programs and reserve hardware and data-files.

So far, we have described different levels of recovery within the *computer system*, which we take to include:

-     central hardware and peripherals
-     environmental equipment: power supply, air conditioning, etc
-     communications equipment, lines and terminals
-     software and application programs
-     data files and program libraries
-     central system operators, and remote terminal operators
-     other people directly concerned with running the computer, eg engineers, librarians, data controllers.

This needs to be distinguished from the *information system* of which it is only a part. A computer system is capable only of a restricted, mechanical class of data-processing activities. In its wider sense, an information system is composed of people giving and obeying instructions, sending and receiving letters and telephone calls, holding meetings, making decisions, forming conclusions and opinions, estimating and guessing, having inspirations; in fact, transforming data in a host of ways which are impossible for a computer.

When a system fails, it may not be able to resolve the failure within itself, but may have to seek the help of some higher-level system. Thus, a failure in the computer may have effects in the information system at large. It then becomes, in a sense, a 'public' failure rather than a private one. It remains private if no incorrect output is delivered to the users of the computer, and service is not interrupted long enough to inconvenience them. To return to the invoice example, if the incorrect invoices produced by a computer failure are spotted in time and if the job is rerun without too much delay, nobody outside the computer system need know about the failure or be involved in recovery. If some of the bad invoices were actually sent to the customers, recovery within the computer system alone is no longer possible. The accounts department – the information system which the computer serves – will have to deal with telephone calls from irate customers, make out corrected invoices by hand and send them off with letters of apology.

Recovery at this level is, for the most part, outside the scope of this book, which is concerned mainly with the computer system. We need to be aware of the information system, however, and of a still higher level of system which is the company or organisation which the computer serves. Its nature, the business or activities in which it engages, and the needs of its customers, largely determine what we mean by reliability and integrity in the computer system. This we shall see in the next section.

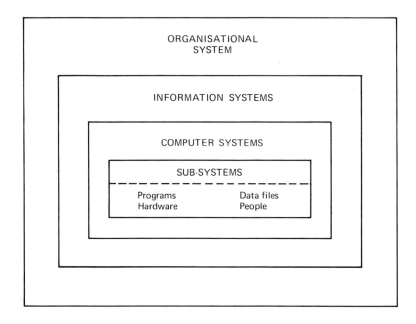

2.2   System levels

2.2 Reliability and integrity

It is generally agreed that computer systems should be *reliable* and should have *integrity*, but people rarely agree about precisely what they mean by those terms. Different aspects of the system's behaviour are emphasized, according to its purpose and the needs of the people who use it and rely on it. There follow some examples of computer systems in which *reliability* and *integrity* can be understood in a variety of ways.

a)   Part of the test procedure for a new aeroplane is to subject the airframe to an extended fatigue test, in which stresses are applied to simulate the effect of many years of actual operation. Hydraulic jacks, heating, cooling and pressurization plant are driven and monitored by mini-computers executing a pre-defined schedule of tests. The full test programme lasts for months and even years. It can be broken off and resumed, so that interruptions of a few hours due to computer failures are not critical. However, as the airframe accumulates thousands of hours of simulated flight, it becomes more and more valuable. If it were to be damaged by applying an excessive stress, much of the previous work would be rendered useless. The computer control and monitoring system must be designed to make sure that this does not happen.

b)   A university time-sharing computer provides a service to a wide variety of students and teaching staff. The files and programs developed by the users are for the most part quite small and concern nobody but the originator. If the system goes down, a number of files may be lost, especially those that were being created at the time of the failure. However, a user can request the system to save a file, when it will make a secure copy of it and will subsequently reproduce it on request.

c)   An on-line computer system assists air traffic controllers to maintain current information about planes leaving and approaching a busy airport. The volume of traffic is so high at peak times that it is nearly impossible for human controllers to keep track of all the aircraft without the aid of the computer. If it were to break down for only a minute, or if it were to 'lose' an airliner, chaos would ensue.

d)   A large, central computer is connected to a network of many hundreds of terminals located in the branch offices of a bank. Trans-actions to be applied to customers' accounts are entered through the terminals during the day. They are validated and stored, to be sorted and processed overnight. If there is a short interruption in service, the operators will wait for a few minutes and catch up with the backlog when the centre is back in service. If the interruption is prolonged, the terminals can be switched to an alternative mode of operation in which they write transactions onto magnetic tape cassettes for later trans-mission. An hour out of service is inconvenient, but not disastrous. However, the system processes about a million transactions a day, each of which represents a sum of money. Any of them might be worth £10 million as easily as £10, and it is vital that no transaction ever be lost.

Each of these examples shows different aspects of reliability or integrity. Let us try to find some of the factors which contribute.

Availability

The most obvious characteristic of a reliable system is that, most of the time, it is available and operating normally. That is to say, it does not break down very often and, when it does, it can be fixed quickly. What do we mean, though, by "not very often" and "quickly"? We can measure availability by two terms borrowed from the engineering world:

– *Mean Time Before Failure* (MTBF)
– *Mean Time To Repair* (MTTR)

MTBF is the average length of time a system will run before it breaks down. MTTR explains itself. *Availability* is the proportion of the total time scheduled for operation that the system is actually available for normal service, and:

Availability = (MTBF)/(MTBF + MTTR)

The phrase "mean time *between* failures" is sometimes used. This *includes* the time to repair, so it is important to know which is meant by the abbreviation MTBF. The first-given interpretation is used throughout this book.

Availability is expressed as a percentage or as a ratio – for example, 95% or 0.95. A quoted availability figure should be treated with care. It may represent frequent interruptions of short duration or infrequent failures which take a long time to repair. Thus, an average of one three minute break in every hour gives an availability of 95%, but so does an average of one full day out per month (of 20 working days). The same availability represents two quite different patterns of behaviour. Which is more acceptable depends on the requirements of the users. If one knows that, once the system has failed, it is going to take several hours to repair, one may be able to put suitable back-up plans into effect, whereas frequent, trifling failures may prove extremely disruptive.

Graceful degradation

A computer system may sometimes be able to limp along in a restricted mode of operation even though some components have failed. The users would often rather accept a degraded service than see the system collapse all at once. The ability to provide a limited service when the system is damaged but not completely stopped is called *graceful degradation*. Operation may continue with longer response times or reduced through-put, as when the system is running on a reduced configuration after a hardware failure. If a program fails or part of the database is temporarily lost, some kinds of transaction may be refused while others are still accepted. In example (d) above, a limited service is provided by allowing transactions to be entered locally, although the central computer is out of action. Generally, operation is only allowed to continue if no further damage is likely to be caused.

Fail-safety

The airframe example (a) illustrates a system which must be *fail-safe*. Whatever else the stress simulation does, it must under no circumstances be allowed to damage the airframe. The common factor in fail-safe systems is that, however they fail, there are certain potentially disastrous things which must definitely *not* be allowed to happen. This is a typical requirement in, for example, process control, where incorrect outputs from the computer can cause expensive damage to machinery and perhaps danger to human life.

Data integrity

This is the ability of the system to prevent errors in its data-base, to detect them as early as possible and correct them or confine their effects. It includes the interception of errors in input data to prevent them ever finding their way into the files. An error can be an item of data with an incorrect value, or the loss of a data item. The banking example (d) shows an extreme requirement for data integrity. No error in the database must ever go undetected, nor any input transaction ever be permanently lost. In practice, of course, the data are never completely error-free. The important factor is the ability to detect and correct the errors. The university time-sharing system (b) has a less rigorous approach to data integrity, in that some current files may be lost after a failure, and the responsibility for recreating them is placed on the users.

System integrity

Another aspect of integrity is the ability of the computer system to detect faults *in its own operation*, and to correct them or at least to limit the damage they cause. If it detects a fault, the system may either shut itself down in an orderly way or attempt to confine the fault to prevent further damage. Faulty programs, for example, must be stopped before they affect other programs or corrupt the database. This aspect of integrity is particularly important in systems whose resources are shared by a variety of users, each of whom expects to be protected from the mistakes of the others – eg time sharing services.

Recovery capability

This is the most important factor of all in reliability and integrity; whatever kind of difficulties the system gets into, it must be possible to get it out again, in a reasonable time and at acceptable cost. However unlikely the contingency, there *must* be a recovery method. The first lesson the novice systems analyst learns is that events that he regarded as virtually impossible almost always happen.

Taken together, the factors listed above are what we mean by reliability and integrity, and they can be restated quite simply. Certain kinds of failure must never occur, and other kinds should happen as rarely as possible. When the system does fail, it must *always* be possible to repair it, and the quicker the better. These requirements are expressed in different terms in each company or organisation. In any particular case, the right approach to integrity and the most appropriate recovery methods can only be selected on a clear understanding of what is important to the organisation in the behaviour of the computer system.

Exercises

1(a) Table 2.1 summarizes the reliability of the major hardware units in a computer system, over a three-month period. For each type of component, work out the MTBF, MTTR and availability averaged over the whole period.

Unit	Total hours scheduled			Number of failures			Total hours lost		
	June	July	Aug	June	July	Aug	June	July	Aug
CPU	420	440	400	2	1	0	5	3	0
I/O channel	420	440	400	3	1	2	8	4	3
Disk drives (4 units)	1680	1760	1600	9	11	5	18	24	7
Tape drives (6 units)	2520	2640	2400	8	9	12	22	24	34

Table 2.1 Unit reliability

1(b) The computer system can adapt to the failure of a tape drive, but if any other unit fails, the whole system stops. Assuming that no 'two failures occurred at the same time, what is the total computer system time lost because of hardware failures in the three months? Neglecting other types of failure, what availability does this give for the computer system as a whole?

2 In the preceding section, several aspects of reliability and integrity were described. What do you think of their relative importance in the computer systems mentioned below? Are any other factors involved?

– An airline seat reservation system.
– A system controlling a continuous-flow chemical manufacture process.
– A commercial computer service bureau.

2.3   Some important subsystems

In any computer system, the mechanisms and responsibility for integrity and recovery are distributed to many different programs, files, hardware devices, procedures and people. We cannot isolate an 'integrity/recovery system' as a distinct subdivision of the computer system, as we can a data management system or an executive program. There are, however, several clearly identifiable jobs which have to be done and which define what we can loosely regard as subsystems:

– system supervision;
– activity recording;
– investigation and decision;

- repair and recovery;
- maintenance and improvement.

System supervision

It is by no means trivial to decide whether a computer system is working properly or not. The system does not always oblige by printing informative error messages, or by behaving in an obviously eccentric way. The internal operation of the computer system must be monitored constantly in order to detect errors as early as possible, *before* they cause serious damage. One can speak informally of the *monitor* as the program or collection of routines responsible for supervising system operation.

We expect errors from four major sources – from hardware faults, program faults, incorrect data and human mistakes. The monitor must intercept errors from all these possible directions, record information about them for future action, and take whatever immediate corrective or protective action it can. It should:

- supervise application programs to ensure that they conform to the rules of the system;
- supervise the allocation of system resources and resolve conflicts, shortages or deadlocks;
- supervise retrieval of records from the database and check for errors; isolate errors and prevent further damage;
- control the quality of incoming data;
- deal with errors notified by application programs and which they cannot handle themselves;
- verify the actions of central site and remote terminal operators and tell them of possible mistakes;
- whenever possible, retrieve control from the operating system after a failure;
- carry out periodic off-line checks on the database.

When the monitor detects an error, it may tell a human operator or it may try to take action on its own. This could include locking out part of the database, suspending certain terminals or programs, or even closing down the entire system.

Activity recording

A variety of information must be recorded about the procesing activity of the system, to support integrity and recovery functions. Some of this is recorded continuously on journals of one kind or another, some of it consists of periodic 'snapshots' of the system, in the form of file dumps or checkpoints. The main purpose of recording the changing state of processing is to provide a basis for recovery from possible future failures; it may also be useful in diagnosing the cause of the failure and, digested in statistical form, in improving the effectiveness and performance of the recovery procedures.

Investigation and decision

When the computer system fails, the problem arises of finding out what is wrong and what can be done about it, and deciding on a course of action. Initially, one may only have the barest information about the failure, and one may need to investigate further to find out why the system failed and how much damage was caused. On the basis of what one discovers, one has to work out a strategy for recovery and, if possible for continuing operation in alternative ways until normal service can be restored. One is engaged in analysis, diagnosis, assessment of priorities and planning, and it is probable that investigation and decision will be largely a human function, with relatively little automatic help from the computer.

Repair and recovery

Following investigation of the cause of a computer system failure, one forms a plan for recovery. This is put into effect by a combination of human effort and computer procedures, and it involves:

- repairing or replacing defective hardware components or computer programs;
- altering the database to correct known errors and to discard updates which cannot be relied on;
- resetting the state of programs;
- telling central and remote terminal operators what to do during recovery, and checking for mistakes;
- restarting programs and restoring normal service.

Maintenance and improvement

Errors contain valuable information which should be collected and analyzed, with a view to improving the system so that they do not recur. This objective is an important one, but it is easy to lose sight of it in the panic to get the system back into service. It is equally important to collect data on the performance of the recovery programs and procedures, both on their speed and on their effectiveness. Some areas in which this information might be useful are:

- modifications or enhancements to hardware or software;
- routine maintenance procedures for hardware or software;
- administrative and operational procedures;
- documentation, manuals and training;
- tuning the recovery procedures for faster recovery.

2.4 A model of an on-line system

In this section, a simple model of an on-line system is developed to provide a suitable framework for the integrity and recovery functions outlined above. The way in which a system is actually implemented depends, of course, on the equipment available and the software it supports, as well as the inclinations of the individual designer. There are various ideas of what constitutes a 'job', a 'program' or a 'process'; a 'file', a 'data-set' or a 'database'. Different computer manufacturers have different packages, facilities and terminology. Nevertheless, there are certain essential control functions which have to be exercised in a real-time system, whatever the details of putting them into effect.

Classes of software

The software in an on-line system is often classified as follows:

- – application programs which do work for the ultimate users of the system; applying transactions, answering enquiries, analyzing data, performing calculations, producing reports;
- – supervisory and control programs which co-ordinate the activities of the application programs and provide common service routines for them; these programs are often called *middleware*;
- – support programs not actually part of the on-line system, but which are used in off-line housekeeping and maintenance;
- – operating system software which administers the hardware resources and provides basic facilities for all the other programs.

In general, application programs only have a limited, local ability to detect and recover from errors. Anything outside their competence has to be notified to the supervisory and control programs. Most integrity and recovery functions are located here, as they are for the most part common to all the application programs. Some elementary error detection and recovery facilities are usually supplied by the operating system. It is, for example, responsible in the first instance for trapping failures in program execution. However, the recovery action it takes is usually directed at preserving its own integrity rather than that of the on-line application system, and any more specific recovery attempt must be made by the on-line system's own supervisory software.

Supervisory functions

Diagram 2.3 shows a possible structure for the supervisory software in which it is divided into three major subsystems. They are responsible for data-communications, database management, and program scheduling and control (the 'executive' subsystem).

The data-communications subsystem is responsible for initiating and controlling transmission of messages to the terminal network and reception of incoming messages:

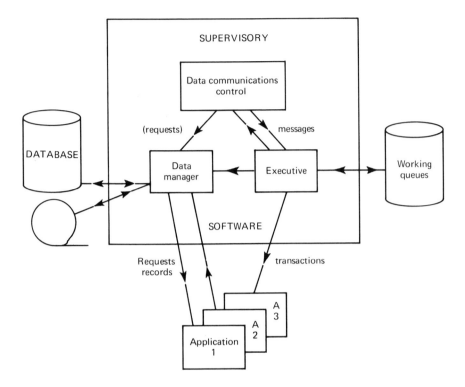

2.3   On-line supervisory software

- it assembles information received over the lines into complete messages and edits and translates them where necessary;
- it recognizes and responds to special control characters and messages;
- it checks for errors and missing transmissions;
- it routes incoming messages to their destination programs;
- it accepts outgoing messages from programs, breaks them down into transmissible form and inserts control and error-checking information.

It also has to manage resources such as main and disk storage for message queues, and it may be responsible for other tasks such as network control, statistics collection, security and some aspects of recovery.

Not all of the functions described above are necessarily performed by programs running in the main computer. Much of the detailed work of assembling, formatting and checking messages may be done in a communications processor specially designed for the job. Sometimes these are hard-wired, which is to say that the logic is fixed in the hardware of the machine. Most modern communications controllers are programmable, however, so that changes to line procedures or new types of terminal can be accommodated more easily.

One point should be noted about the structure illustrated in diagram 2.3. The data-communications system does not deal directly with application programs; rather, all messages are routed through the executive subsystem. This is not essential, but it does have some advantages for central control over work scheduling.

The executive program is responsible for overall control of the whole system. It schedules and initiates application programs, distributes work to them and monitors their progress. It may also carry out some preliminary validation on transactions before handing them over. It provides common service routines to the aplications, and handles exceptional conditions which they are unable to deal with themselves. The executive communicates with the system operators, tells them about situations which require their intervention, and checks for mistakes when they enter instructions.

The last major subsystem is the data manager, which controls access to the database. All requests from application programs to retrieve or store data are directed to the data-manager. It may be a relatively simple program supervising a set of ordinary files, or it may be a full-scale database management system. This is not the place to go into a discussion of what is or is not a DBMS; the important point about the structure described here is that all access to the data is through a single, central subsystem. Individual application programs are not allowed to get directly at the data-base. This is practically essential from the recovery point of view, as we shall see.

Some of the functions performed by the data-manager might be:

- converting requests from applications into physical I/O operations on the files;
- searching indexes and record lists;
- scheduling I/O operations efficiently;
- resolving conflicts between programs for the use of the same data;
- maintaining and re-organizing the database;
- data compression and expansion, encoding, decoding, translation, editing and reformatting;

Responsibility for integrity and recovery

One of the major integrity and recovery tasks outlined in the previous section was error monitoring and system supervision. The responsibility for this is divided between the three control subsystems we have just described, and forms a major part of their work. The executive is in overall control of all programs in the system – the other supervisory programs as well as the applications programs – and also acts as the main interface with the operators. The data manager supervises all activity on the files, and can detect errors in the data it handles or in the request for application programs. Similarly, activity logging can be achieved jointly by the data-manager and the executive. Database repair and recovery may be carried out largely by off-line support programs, but the last stages before normal service is restored, when application programs are restarted and contact is re-established with the remote terminals, are co-ordinated by the executive with the other supervisory programs under its direction.

Ideally, failure and recovery should be completely invisible to the application programs. This is rarely possible in practice, but it can be approached if the interfaces between an application and the supervisory functions are few and simple. If each application could process the database independently, without overall supervision and co-ordination, it would be virtually impossible to determine which program had updated what and in what order, and recovery would be enormously complicated. Central co-ordination is essential for good recovery procedures. The software structure shown here has that as its main objective. It is by no means the only possibility, but something like it is implicit in most on-line systems.

2.5 Some special problems

There is no doubt that certain types of system and certain approaches to systems design bring more integrity and recovery problems than others. Four particular problem areas are discussed below. They are:

- on-line operation
- updating files in place
- integrated database systems
- large-scale systems

On-line operation

When one speaks of 'real-time' computer systems, one is in danger of confusing a number of integrity and recovery problems which are related but different. First, we consider the special factors involved in *on-line* operation, by which we mean that a significant proportion of the input and output data for the system are transmitted through a data-communications network. Often, the input data are entered directly from source documents at the remote terminal, so that it does not exist in any machine-readable form except as it is received through the on-line network. In a batch system, by contrast, the data are prepared and validated in batches on some physically available medium such as a card deck or a magnetic tape. There are, of course, intermediate types of system such as *remote batch* or *remote job entry*, in which large batches of data are transmitted through a high-speed, on-line terminal, but the simple case is considered here for the sake of example.

When a batch system fails, the input transactions are not usually affected, so they can be submitted again for processing when the system has been repaired. On-line operation immediately complicates the issue. Transactions arrive at random from a network of terminals, and it is not always easy to reproduce them after a failure. They have to be saved on some secure medium as they arrive, in case they are needed later for recovery. There is a chance that some messages may be lost after a failure despite this precaution; one must make sure that terminal operators know what to do so that no transactions are lost permanently or processed twice.

In batch-processing installations, input data are usually verified by an independent operator after they have first been keyed. There is no opportunity to do this when the data are entered on-line, so one must have extra concern for the quality of the input. Balancing this, however, on-line data entry gives the opportunity to check and correct errors at source.

Updating files in place

Perhaps the most important factor in integrity recovery is *the method by which the files are updated*; in particular, there is a very important distinction between:

 – update by generation, in which transactions are applied to the old data creating a new version which is stored separately – on a new reel of tape, or a different area of disc;
 – update in place, in which the new, updated data overwrites and destroys the old version.

The latter method is commonly used in real-time systems which require the most recent, up-to-the-minute information to be instantly available. It is sometimes used in batch systems, however. Many on-line systems use update by generation; they collect the incoming transactions into sizable batches, sort and validate them, and process them sequentially, perhaps when the communications system has closed down overnight. Thus there is no direct association between the file updating technique and the method of collecting the input data.

In what one may call the *classical batch* approach, transactions are applied sequentially to an old master file to create a new generation of it; the old file is unaltered. If there is a failure during an updating run, the old file and the corresponding batch of transactions are usually undamaged. All or part of the new file which was being created is discarded and the run can be started again, from the beginning or some intermediate point. Even if the old master file is unusable, recovery can be based on previous generations and their corresponding transactions. The actual practice may be rather more complicated than this, as we shall see in chapter 5, but the basic principles of recovery are simple.

When the on-line files are updated in place, however, the problems are very different and the recovery techniques are much more complex. Transactions are applied directly to the on-line files, the new information over-writing the old. If system operation is interrupted by a failure, a simple re-run is not possible because the old version of the file no longer exists. A method must be found to correct the files so that the system can be restarted. Moreover, many real-time systems have to provide a virtually continuous service, so that normal operations and recovery must go on side by side.

Integrated database systems

In this book, *database* generally means no more than a collection of files. In this particular case, however, it is taken to have the more specific meaning of a set of integrated files accessible to a group of applications by a common logical access method. It is irrelevant whether the access method is a generalized database management system or something designed specially for the job. Integrated files allow the application programs to correlate data from many different sources and, often, each is allowed to retrieve the data along different access paths and in a variety of relationships. Thus, each element of data may participate in many relationships with other items. This means that it may be very difficult to find errors in the database and unravel their consequences, and they may spread quite rapidly before they are detected.

The ability to see the same data item in various ways from different applications allows one to store an item in one place only whereas, in a conventional file system, one might have to repeat it several times for the benefit of several programs. However, this data redundancy does provide a built-in check against error which is partially lost in an integrated database.

Problems of scale

Sheer size, both of programs and of data files, is in itself a problem from the point of view of integrity and recovery. Large programs are more difficult to construct, test and maintain than small ones, and are likely to contain more undetected faults. Unfortunately, many on-line systems are large and complex, simply because they have a complex job to do.

If we make the conservative assumption that the incidence of errors in data is, on average, proportional to the amount of data stored, large files are bound to be more prone to error than small ones. It inevitably takes longer to reconstruct a large database, unless one can find some way of dividing it into logically independent parts which can be repaired or replaced separately. This in its turn is bound to make the recovery procedures more complicated. In a large database one may find that some of the data are only accessed very rarely, and that errors accumulate until they are detected months or even years after their first occurrence.

In conclusion, none of the problems mentioned above are insuperable, and some of them are avoidable. One can either accept the cost of solving them, or one can avoid them by adopting a design which may fall short of the ideal in other respects. However, the arguments for real-time systems or integrated databases have often turned out to be based on technical infatuation or corporate one-upmanship rather than on real needs. One of the systems designer's principal aims in life should be to keep things as simple as possible, and he should only take on problems if he can see very compelling reasons to do so. If the technical and business justification is sound, then face them he must.

Chapter 3

Faults, errors and failures

3.1 Faults and failures: cause and effect

We can do nothing about the failure of a computer system until we know that it *has* failed. The breakdown may become apparent in a number of ways:

  – the system detects a fault in itself, tells the operators, and either shuts down in an orderly fashion, or attempts to carry on as best it can;
  – it starts misbehaving in an obvious way, by producing visibly incorrect output, working very slowly or stopping altogether;
  – it generates wrong output which is not discovered until it reaches the user, who complains.

Certain kinds of fault are immediately and plainly identifiable, and there is no difficulty in deciding why the system has broken down. Failures of the power supply or of major hardware units come into this category. Other kinds have subtler effects which do not appear for some time. By the time the failure becomes evident, it is not at all clear where the fault lies, nor when it occurred, nor how much damage it caused.

Here is an example of how a fault may not make itself felt until some time after its first occurrence. While processing a transaction, a program reads some records from the database, updates them, and writes them back. However, the unit on which they are kept is faulty, and stores them incorrectly. The next time a transaction applying to those records is received – which could be within minutes, but perhaps not until days later – they are retrieved again. This time, the processing program finds the errors and is unable to deal with them, and there is a system failure.

To avoid confusion, the words *fault,* *error* and *failure* are used here with different and specific meanings. A *fault* is a malfunction in a hardware, software or human component of the system, which may introduce or allow to be introduced *errors*. These are items of data or pieces of program incorrectly stored or transmitted within the system, or lost altogether. In due course, an error may cause a *failure*, which is cessation of normal, timely operation by all or part of the system, or delivery to the outside world of incorrect data. Sometimes the fault and the failure are simultaneous, as in the case of a major hardware breakdown, but it is still useful to draw the distinction.

When the computer system fails, we have a number of objectives:

- to find the error which was the immediate cause of the failure;
- to locate the original fault, and find out when it first occurred;
- to discover the full extent of damage to the database, programs, equipment, storage media, and of incorrect results delivered to the users.

We have also to decide on a strategy for recovery, which will include:

- repairing the fault and the damage it caused;
- restoring normal service;
- 'getting round' the failure, ie continuing some kind of service while repairs are in progress.

There may be some hard detective work to be done in diagnosing the original fault. If it is a hardware problem, some help might be had from diagnostic software or test equipment, which exercises the functions of the machine to find out which components are working properly and which are not. Locating software faults is usually more difficult. It often depends on the intuition, patience and experience of the maintenance programmer.

One employs a variety of methods to find a 'bug' in a computer program. Some of them are based on logic, and can be learned and used systematically; others are less scientific. Given enough knowledge about the operating system and the way it organizes programs in main storage, one can extract a good deal of information from a core-dump, according to a fixed prescription. A certain location may hold a pointer to a list of starting addresses for programs in execution; at a fixed displacement from each of these, one may find a table of program segment addresses; from the error message printed when the system failed, one can find out which program was running; from its compilation listing, some simple arithmetic tells exactly what the program was doing when it failed; and so on.

This is all very logical. A more intuitive approach is exemplified by 'looking at a print of the file to see if anything looks a bit odd'. One can actually do this with some success, and rationalize about it afterwards, but it is virtually impossible to explain in advance exactly what one expects to find.

In the case of the storage unit failure mentioned above, the process of diagnosis might run as follows. The programmer responsible has a core dump taken when the system fails, and takes a copy of the console messages. The console log tells him the immediate cause of the failure. The application program was terminated by the operating system when it tried to access an invalid data item. Looking at the dump and tracing through the pointers and control tables, he finds the offending program and the bad data that it was trying to process, and he discovers the identity of the corrupted record. He orders a print-out of the area of the file in its immediate vicinity and finds that one complete track of the disk is bad, and designs the recovery procedure accordingly.

Some of this is quite straightforward and could be done automatically. However, the example was chosen for its simplicity, and in practice it is unlikely that one could ever dispense with the intuition of the human programmer completely. Many of the faults which occur in real-time systems are transient, depending on particular combinations of events and input data. They may be extremely difficult to reproduce, and if they are ever traced at all, it is usually as a result of ingenuity or inspired guesswork.

The most important objective after a system failure is to restore normal operation. One is usually more interested in getting the system back into service than in conducting detailed post-mortems, and quite often this can be done without ever finding out what caused the failure. The effort devoted to diagnosis must depend on one's priorities. One may, for example, regard the accuracy of the database as vitally important. Lengthy interruptions to service may be preferable to the risk of further damage caused by undetected faults. Some faults, however, are so difficult to trace and so rare that it is worth no-one's while to pursue them. The pressures of data-processing life being what they are, many of these mysteries have to remain unsolved.

3.2   Faults in computer systems

There are a number of different ways one can classify faults in a computer system. Martin (1) and Yourdon (2) each have classifications of their own. In this section, however, six basic types are described:

- inadequate input validation
- design miscalculation
- system control faults
- hardware faults
- software faults
- human mistakes.

Inadequate input validation

The exact specification of all the types and ranges of input which the system is expected to process is an essential part of its definition. Validation is supposed to trap all illegal input data and reject them. If it allows bad data to slip through there is a good chance that the application programs will produce incorrect results, insert errors into the database, or break down completely. The simpler kinds of input error – missing, mispunched or transposed characters, missing transactions – can be detected relatively easily. More subtle errors may not be anticipated by the systems designer, and he may omit to build in checks for them.

Design miscalculation

A computer system must have adequate safety margins built into it to enable it to cope with exceptional conditions. The loads it has to handle may include sharp, short-term peaks, sustained, long-term peaks and unusual distributions of transactions. They may be due to purely random variation, or to regular patterns of activity, such as the rush of business in a bank during the lunch-hour. Any unusual load may strain the processing or storage capacity of the system. A well-designed system should have the flexibility to cope with such variations without any serious effects. The standard of service may suffer for a while, but it should recover as soon as the load has returned to its normal level. In a poorly designed system, the capacity of the machine may be inadequate for it to catch up. This is a fundamental fault, however, which can generally only be cured by more powerful equipment or basic redesign. A more subtle fault is that the system may lose incoming data when it is overloaded.

System control faults

The resources of the computer system are managed partly by the operating system and partly by the user's own control software. The logic of either may be faulty in a way which results in inefficient operation or total failure. Poor task scheduling, poor storage management and dead-locks are three examples, which are explained below.

A real-time system is composed of a number of programs which are competing for the use of the main processor. The operating system, or an executive program, decides which program to schedule next on the basis of priorities. These are partly determined by the importance of the job done by the programs – for example, some transactions are more urgent than others – and partly by the need to use the whole hardware system efficiently. However, the algorithm which schedules and despatches programs may allow high priority programs to block out those of lower priority completely. Under certain load conditions, some kinds of trans-actions will get no service at all.

There is not usually enough main storage space to allow every program in the system to be in core at the same time, so special routines are needed to allocate pieces of it as required and to make it available again when a program has finished using it. After the system has been running for some time, 'checkerboarding' may develop. The available storage is broken up into many small, scattered segments which make it difficult to find and allocate areas of the right size. At first, this is merely inefficient, but finally it may be impossible to satisfy a request for space from a user program, and the system fails.

In a multiprogramming computer, a number of processes are in competition for a limited supply of resources. Processing time and main storage space are two such resources, as we have just seen. Peripheral devices and data files are two more. Some of them can only be used by one process at a time, and have to be *locked* to prevent others from using them. To complete its task, a process may need to secure the use of several resources, some of which are also wanted by other processes. This can cause a situation called *deadlock*, of which diagram 3.1 shows a simple example. Process A has locked resource 1, but cannot continue until it has resource 2, which has already been locked by process B. B, however, is waiting for A to release resource 1. Neither process can continue, and it may be some time before the deadlock is discovered.

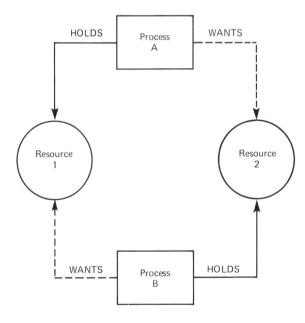

3.1   Deadlock

Deadlock, checkerboarding and similar conditions are incorrect states of the system. They can be regarded as errors in the same way as lost transactions or corrupted records in the database. They are caused by faulty control software design, and can exist for some time without noticeable effect, until finally they cause a failure. It is quite consistent, therefore, to extend the definition of errors to include *incorrect control states*.

Hardware faults

Any component of the hardware system may develop a fault, including:

- the central processor and its main memory
- auxiliary input-output processors and channels
- peripheral devices and their control units
- storage media: disk packs and tape volumes
- data-communications processors or controllers
- communications lines, terminals, modems, multiplexors, concentrators
- environmental equipment: air conditioning, power supply, etc.

Some components are more reliable than others. A central processor, for example, is protected in a clean, controlled computer room, and is regularly maintained. It is likely to be far less prone to error than a communications line, which is buried in the ground and is subject to electrical interference, corrosion and vibration. However, we must examine what we mean by 'reliable'. Telephone lines rarely break down completely, so their MTBF might be measured in years. A more realistic measure is the frequency with which it transmits an incorrect bit of information. For an ordinary voice-grade line transmitting at 2400 bits per second, a typical figure is one error in every 100,000 bits (Martin, 3).

Program faults

Computer programs are written by people and, like people, they are never perfect. This is as true, unfortunately, of systems software as it is of user-written programs. Faults may be introduced into programs at any stage of their lives:

- during specification; the analyst may omit to specify what a program should do under certain circumstances, and the programmer may omit to ask. As implemented, the program may either do the wrong thing or do nothing at all;
- in design; the processing algorithms chosen to do a particular job may be wrong, in that they fail to reflect real life;
- in implementation; through carelessness, or misunderstanding, or lack of testing, the programmer may not code what is required;

   – in maintenance; while enhancing the program or correcting
     known faults in it, new faults may be introduced as unexpected
     side-effects.

The larger and more complex a program is, the more faults it is likely to
have. A large program can be very difficult to maintain, since on average
correcting a fault may cause more problems than it cures. The faults in
some large operating systems and data management packages are numbered in thousands, and the number increases with time rather than
diminishes. The subject of program complexity and reliability is a wide
one. For the reader who wants to pursue it further, there is a paper by
Crandon and Anderson (4) which contains a large number of references.

Human mistakes

The last major source of error in the computer system is the human
operator. The central operators are asked to make decisions which the
programs cannot make and have no means of verifying, and the scope for
disaster if they decide wrongly is considerable. Some of the mistakes they
can make are:

   – mounting the wrong versions of files
   – using the wrong versions of programs
   – responding incorrectly to console messages from the operating
     system or user programs
   – overriding normal operation of the system by, for example,
     purging files or aborting programs
   – damaging data volumes by careless handling.

This presents a rather bleak picture of the computer operator, which is
not what is intended. Because of his position of on-the-spot responsibility
and his direct access to the computer, however, he can cause a great deal
of damage if he does make a mistake.

The central operators are not the only people with the opportunity to
introduce errors. Incorrect data entered by the remote terminal operators
ought to be trapped by input validation, but this is not always foolproof.
The librarians or data controllers may issue the wrong file volumes or
may lose or damage them.

The author's experience also includes a computer engineer who left a
loose plug in a disk drive in such an ingenious way that, while the
operating system thought a record was being written, no data were
actually transferred. The capacity of people to invent new ways of
causing chaos defies the imagination of even the most pessimistic systems
designer.

3.3 System failures

A failure, as we have defined it, is when the computer system completely
or partially ceases normal operation, or when it delivers incorrect output

to the outside world. Failures come in various degrees of severity. The whole system may break down, or only a small part of it. It may stop completely, or limp along at reduced speed. Five types of failure are described below:

- machine failures
- program failures
- overload failures
- database access failures
- data validity failures.

As we have already noted, failures are caused by faults, and our main interest in classifying a failure is so that we can find out what caused it and how it can be repaired. Before we can even classify it, though, we have to make the simple observation that the system has failed. The evidence for this may be an informative error message printed on the console; it may be a telephone call from a user whose terminal has lost contact; it may be a suspicious silence from the computer room. Our first concern is to find the immediate cause of the failure rather than its origin and history.

Machine failures

Machine failures occur when there are hardware faults sufficiently persistent or severe to prevent normal processing. As we have already seen, a hardware fault is not the same as a machine failure, since some faults have no immediate effect at the time of their first occurrence; they may cause a completely different kind of failure much later.

A machine failure need not cripple the entire system. One may be able to withdraw non-critical devices from service and replace them with reserve units, or do without them altogether. A disk drive failure may stop the programs which need to access the data stored on it, but other programs may continue without interruption.

When an irreplaceable major unit such as the central processor fails, then so does the entire system. However, in some advanced multi-processor systems, special hardware and software facilities automatically transfer the load to whatever units have survived. This is called *automatic reconfiguration*.

Program failures

These failures happen when a program attempts to perform an illegal operation of some kind. This usually causes a hardware interrupt, which stops the offending program and transfers control to the operating system. Among the possible types are:

- arithmetic errors; division by zero, overflow, underflow;

- data format errors; eg attempts to use character data as numeric; on some machines, executable code cannot be used as data, nor vice-versa;

- violation of storage protection rules; attempting to use another program's area of store, to index beyond the declared bounds of an array, or to violate addressing restrictions for instructions;

- attempts to execute invalid instructions, or those restricted for privileged use by the operating system.

These failures may occur in application or supervisory programs, or even in the operating system itself, while it is doing some work for a user program. The operating system may fail through some fault in its own code, but it is more likely that the user program passed some invalid parameters to it. Thus, programs which want the operating system to open a file, or read or write a record, pass over the address of a control block which contains all the relevant information about the file. The operating system knows the format of a control block, and supposes that that is what it has been given. If the address or the format of the data itself is invalid, the operating system will probably fail, and if it succeeds in recovering it will terminate the program which caused the failure.

Program failures generally derive from incorrect data or program code in main memory, where they may have been corrupted by a hardware fault or a logic fault in this or some other program. Alternatively, the data may have been transferred incorrectly from a secondary storage device, perhaps some time before the failure, and this, too, can happen equally to data records or to segments of code from the program libraries.

Initially, program failures are handled by the operating system, and in the absence of any instructions to the contrary, it will print an error message at the console and terminate the program. It may, however, be able to return control to the failed program, if requested. There are facilities in many operating systems which allow a user program to specify action of its own after certain kinds of failure. The program is interrupted as before, but this time the operating system passes control back to a special routine in the user program. The ON-condition facility in the PL/1 programming language (5) is a good example of how this may be put into effect. After retrieving control, the user program may take some recovery action of its own, or it may simply print more extensive information about the failure before coming to an end.

Overload failures

Overload failures happen when the system is subjected to a volume of work for which it was not designed, either because of exceptional peak loads or because of design miscalculation. It may stop altogether, or performance may deteriorate to unacceptable levels.

One way in which the system can fail is through lack of space. Certain operating systems allocate a fixed amount of core to each program at the start of its run, and if the user program requests more than its allowance, it is terminated. Even with more flexible forms of storage management, the physical limits of the hardware may be reached, and if no space can be released by other tasks, a failure cannot be avoided. Similarly, user programs may exceed limits designed into them, by overflowing the limits of control tables or temporary working files; recovery may involve redefining the limits and recompiling the programs.

Depending on the types of terminal attached to the network and the line disciplines used to control them, it is sometimes possible to control the rate at which messages are accepted by the central system. If this is the case queues of outstanding work can be kept waiting at the remote terminals while the centre processes messages as fast as it can. Otherwise, the centre may find itself swamped by transactions which arrive faster than it can deal with them, and breakdown begins at critical points or bottlenecks in the system.

The first sign of breakdown is that queues of messages or requests waiting for service at the most overworked units or programs grow excessively long. They may grow to fill all the available main storage space. At this point, the system may give up altogether or it may resort to spilling the queues onto auxiliary storage. There may now be such a sharp degradation in performance, because of the overheads involved in managing the queues on disk or drum, that the system never again catches up with the backlog of work. The reasons for the sudden deterioration lie in the mathematical theory of the behaviour of queues; Martin (3) gives a good summary of the parts of this which are relevant to real-time systems design.

The trade-off between available space and performance is a common one. It is seen very clearly in the behaviour of virtual-storage computers. These are machines which provide what appears to user programs to be a very large addressable storage space, but which actually make do with a smaller real main store which is managed and allocated by the operating system and hardware. This is achieved by dividing the virtual, or apparent, space into *pages* or *segments*, which are sometimes in real memory and sometimes on a backing storage device such as a high-speed disk or drum, waiting to be read in when next referred to. The transfer of pages between real and backing store is known as *paging* or *overlaying*. If the limited amount of real space is too heavily used, the paging overheads become very high, and beyond a certain point performance deteriorates rapidly. The system is spending most of its time paging and scarcely any doing useful work.

This phenomenon is called *thrashing*. It is characteristic of systems in which there are queues for service at components or for resources which are near or beyond their maximum capacity, and is very similar to the behaviour of a real-time system running under excessive load. In many real-time systems there is a danger that only a small increase in message traffic may cause a disproportionately sharp increase in response time and reduction in throughput.

Database access failures

These arise when the data manager is unable to satisfy a user program's request for an operation on the database. There are a number of possible reasons:

- error conditions such as incorrect parity, unexpected end of file or invalid retrieval key make a record unavailable;

- required records are missing or invalid, or contain invalid pointers or other structural information;

- the user program has made an invalid request; for example, to write a record it did not previously request to be locked and read;

- two or more users may end up in deadlock while attempting to update the same records.

Data validity failures

Even if records in the database are correctly stored and retrieved, there is no guarantee that the information they contain is correct. The data manager is responsible for storing records at the request of application programs, and returning them in the same condition in which it received them. It is not usually concerned with the external interpretation of the data, and has no way of checking the validity of the application information, although it may be able to do some elementary validation of its format. An application program can ascribe some meaning to the data, and may discern errors there which are invisible to the data management system. If the errors are beyond its competence to handle, it may fail or it may notify the supervisory software and wait for further instructions.

3.4 Failure during recovery

Perhaps the most awkward time for a system failure is during recovery from a previous breakdown. Since, in effect, one line of the system's defences has already been broken, this can be very serious. Unless the recovery procedures take account of the possibility that they themselves may fail, a relatively trivial problem may turn into a major disaster.

It is quite common for failures to happen in rapid succession; before the recovery programs can restart the system after the first stoppage, another brings it down again. Faults in the hardware or software may not be diagnosed correctly at first, nor do the attempted repairs always succeed. It is easy to disturb other hardware units while fixing a faulty component, or to introduce new faults into a program while supposedly correcting it. There may also be errors in the database which were not discovered prior to the recovery attempt.

Aside from the applications database, the integrity and recovery routines maintain a good deal of information of their own, which they use during recovery. This includes *journals* and *logs, checkpoint files,* special *restart files* and *directories.* These are used, as we shall see in later chapters, partly for database reconstruction and partly for controlling the restart operation. They are vital for successful recovery. However, they are just as likely to be damaged as the applications files themselves, by program and hardware faults and operator mistakes. Destruction of the restart data may have catastrophic consequences, so they must be protected with extreme care.

It is an unfortunate fact that recovery procedures – by which we mean operational procedures as well as programs – are often not tested as thoroughly as the rest of the system. This is understandable, since it can be very difficult to reproduce the conditions of failure systematically enough to test the procedures properly. It means that there is a fair chance of a recovery program failing under circumstances which have never been met before, and for which the operators have neither instructions nor training.

The operators on the spot have a great responsibility when the system fails. Ideally, they should be fully trained and provided with detailed manuals telling them what to do in an emergency, which they actually know how to use. Real life is rarely like the training manuals, however. Decisions and action have to be taken under pressure, with managers, liaison staff and perhaps hundreds of users all anxiously demanding to know what is going on and how soon it can be fixed. The best-trained people, in full possession of their faculties, are likely to make mistakes under these conditions. Worse, the system is quite likely to collapse at 3am, in the charge of a sleepy and inexperienced crew of operators, with the nearest expert help asleep in bed ten miles away. In such a situation, it is easy to make hasty and ill-advised decisions which aggravate the damage done by the original failure.

The moral to be drawn is that it is extremely dangerous to design recovery procedures in the expectation or hope that they will always work first time. It is virtually certain that, at some time in the life of the system, a failure will occur in the middle of recovery, and the designer must be prepared for it. The essential principle is that recovery should always be repeatable. Nothing the restart programs do should prejudice the chances of a subsequent attempt, and they should never expose vital recovery data to danger.

References

1. James Martin, *Security, Accuracy and Privacy in Computer Systems*, Prentice Hall, 1973.
2. Edward Yourdon, *The causes of System Failures*, Modern Data, February 1972.
3. James Martin, *Systems Analysis for Data Transmission*, Prentice Hall, 1972.
4. P G Anderson and L H Crandon, *Computer Program Reliability*, RCA Corporation, 1974. Also published (without references) in Computers and People, July 1974.
5. *PL/1 (F) Language Reference Manual GC28-8201, IBM 1971.*

Chapter 4

Basic strategies

4.1 Error prevention and control

The earlier an error is detected, the less damage it causes and the easier is the task of recovery. As an important part of the overall strategy for integrity and recovery, therefore, one should aim to prevent as many errors as one can, and to monitor the system continually to trap those that do occur as early as possible. The techniques available to achieve this can be classified as:

–   features provided by the hardware and software, over which the system designer has little control;
–   techniques which are at the system designer's own disposal.

The designer is not often in the happy position of being able to choose his own hardware. If he is, he is bound to take into account in his decision or recommendation the ability of the machine and its associated software to detect and correct errors. If, as is more likely, he is obliged to work with the equipment that is already available, all he can do is to use his knowledge of the machine to identify its strengths and weaknesses, to avoid using suspect devices or software, and to provide extra support in the supervisory software where necessary.

In his evaluation, he might look for some of the following facilities:

–   error checking and correction information associated with stored characters and words; parity and modulus check bits; self-correcting character codes (1);
–   checks on complete records and transmitted messages; block check characters and polynomial codes (1);
–   error checking and re-try during CPU instruction execution;
–   ability of channels and device controllers to verify and re-try I/O operations; software facilities to read and verify data records

after writing them;

- communications line control procedures to detect and recover from transmission errors (3);
- main storage protection facilities to prevent programs from interfering with one another; division of store into regions with separate protection keys (4); checking array bounds; identification of store contents by type (data, program code, pointer, etc) to prevent incorrect usage (5, 6); virtual storage management, denying programs access to real storage addresses (6, 7);
- data management software with automatic error checking and data validation facilities.

Input validation and control

The hardware supplier can do his best to ensure that data are preserved intact in storage and in transit from one device to the next, but he can by no means guarantee that the data are sensible when they first come into the system. This is largely the responsibility of the designer.

Thorough input validation is essential for the integrity of the database. The conventional view of it is that it is a process of filtering out bad data. The input is subjected to a set of tests to find out whether it satisfies specific rules for acceptance. Checks are applied to individual characters or fields to make sure that they contain the right type of data and fall within allowed ranges of values; to whole transactions, to test that they are complete and consistent internally and with external reference data; and to batches of transactions. This form of validation is, of course, indispensible, but it is a very wide subject which is impossible to cover here. Martin (1) is recommended as a starting point for more information.

In an on-line system, it is possible to combine the rejection of bad input with an approach which actively encourages the operators to enter good data. The design of the terminal dialogue is crucial in reducing the incidence of input errors. It must be tailored to the skill and experience of the operator in the amount of information it presents to him, the complexity of the decisions it expects him to make, and the pace at which it moves. It can assist the operator, and reduce the opportunity for mistakes, by:

- prompting him for input;
- offering choices from a limited range of alternatives;
- allowing him to check, back-track and change his mind before committing himself;
- asking him for confirmation that his input has been understood correctly;
- telling him of errors and giving him a chance to correct them immediately.

Let us take an on-line order processing system as a simple example. At some stage in each order, the operator is prompted as follows:

QUANTITY, CATALOGUE NO:

He responds:

1000, 41086

And the system sends back:

1000, POLYSTYRENE PELLETS, 100KG DRUMS

The operator spots a mistake, and enters:

X, 1000, 41806

To which the system replies:

CORRECTION
1000, PVC POWDER (ORANGE), 50KG SACKS

The operator confirms that this is correct, and the order proceeds to the next stage. A skilled operator might find it very irritating to be prompted all the time when he knows very well what he is going to enter next, and a more concise form of dialogue would be appropriate for him than for an unskilled operator or for an occasional user of the system. The possibilities have only been outlined here, but for more information on dialogue design, another excellent book by Martin (8) is recommended.

Monitoring the database

However reliable the hardware and software may be, and however thoroughly the input data is validated, some errors are bound to find their way into the database. It has to be monitored constantly to find and correct errors, otherwise they will accumulate and proliferate until the database becomes unusable.

Checks should be applied every time an application program makes a request to retrieve or store a record. This ensures that, so far as can be determined, the data are correct before they are used and again before they are entered in the database, and it also gives a sample of the condition of the database as a whole. The data manager can collect statistics about the frequency and location of errors which may give useful guidance on possible improvements to the system.

One of the more important checks that the data manager should perform is to ensure that a record that it has retrieved is actually the one that it is looking for. This is by no means certain; either hardware or program faults may cause a record to be stored at or retrieved from the wrong address. Application programs ask for data by means of an identifying key, which is transformed by the data manager and its file access methods into a physical address. Suppose that an application program asks for the account record for customer number 410796. The data manager consults a number of tables, indexes and lists and decides that the record is at block number 11483 on disk unit E4. On retrieving what it thinks is the right

record, and on checking the account number stored in it, it finds it to be
200710. Two questions then arise:

- how did 200710 come to be there?
- what happened to 410796, and where is it now?

One of the reasons we keep a journal or audit trail of activity in the
system is to solve detective problems like this, as we shall see.

Some data management systems go beyond checking the parity of the
record and identifying it as the right one, and try to validate it against a
format or prototype of what this kind of record should look like. This is
more usually left to the applications programs, however.

In addition to the information stored for the applications programs,
records may contain structural information such as pointers to other
records. The first indication of an error is often to be found here, for
example:

- in a list of records linked in both directions, a record does not
  point back to the one which pointed to it;
- there is a closed loop in a chain of records;
- a record in a chain does not point to the head of the chain;
- records with similar attributes are linked together in a list, but
  one of them does not have the attributes it is supposed to have;
  for example, in a list of all orders from the same customer, one
  order has the wrong account number.
- a chain does not finish at the header record from which it
  started.

Some of these may be detected accidentally during the course of normal
procesing. Others may require a systematic search through the whole file.
One may, for example, want to check that all records are included in
some chain or other, or that the number of elements in a list is equal to the
number recorded in the head of the list. At intervals, one may run a
program or suite of programs which reads the whole database, or a
relevant subset of it, and systematically checks structural and, where
possible, applications data. This is likely to be a lengthy job which one
might run in spare time at night or over the weekend, or one might do it at
the same time as reorganizing the data base or dumping copies of it.

Detecting and resolving deadlocks

Deadlocks are a serious problem in designing operating systems, which
have to manage a number of processes competing for a wide variety of
resources. General approaches to detecting, avoiding and preventing
deadlocks have been studied by the designers of such systems – see, for
example, Howard (9).

Applications systems designers most commonly meet the problem when there is a need for a number of programs to update the same database concurrently. Two or more programs may reach deadlock when they are trying to update the same records.

As we saw in the last chapter, deadlock only happens when there is a closed loop of resources and processes waiting to use them. One can avoid this by insisting that processes request and lock resources in a fixed

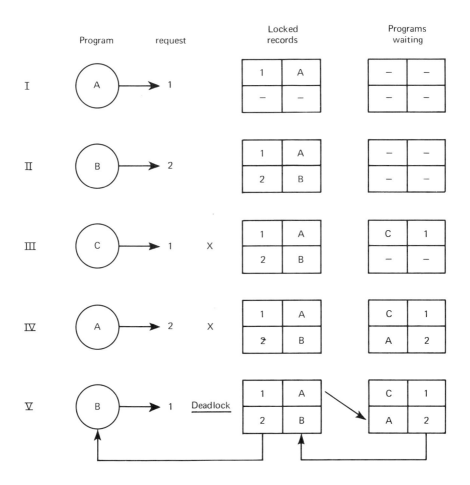

4.1   Detecting deadlocks

order. Thus, one may require that each program requests records first from file A, then from file B, then from C, and so on. Suppose that program 1 starts to request the records it needs to process a transaction, until it finds that a record of file X has already been secured by program 2. It must wait for program 2 to finish with it and release it. However, program 2 cannot go back and ask for any of the files that program 1 has, as they are all earlier in the requesting order than file X. It must release at least the file X record first.

A discipline like this can be used to prevent all deadlocks, if it is possible to apply it. However, it makes life more complicated for the application programmer, and the structure of the transactions may make it difficult or logically impossible to keep to it. Even if it is feasible, it may have an undesirable effect on performance. One is then forced to recognize that deadlocks will occasionally happen, and to provide some way of detecting and resolving them.

A common way of detecting a deadlock is to receive a complaint from a user that nothing has happened at his terminal for ten minutes. If no active steps are taken to look for them, deadlocks can go unnoticed for a considerable time. The data manager can forestall this by imposing time limits for holding records, after which it will examine the holding program to find out why it is waiting. Alternatively, one may check for possible deadlocks every time a request is made to secure a record, as described below and shown in diagram 4.1.

All requests for records are made through the data management system. If a record is needed for update rather than for enquiry, the data manager will make a note of its identity and that of the program to which it is being issued. It will not allow any other program to use it until the first has released it. If another program asks for the locked record, it is put in a waiting queue. As time goes on, a number of records will be locked out and there may be several programs waiting.

Before allowing any program to join the waiting list, however, the system asks:

–   Which program holds the record which the new program wants?
–   Is the holding program now waiting for any other records?
–   Are any of these held by the new program?

If the answer to all of these is "yes", then there is a simple two-program deadlock. More complicated deadlocks involving three or more programs are possible, and these require more exhaustive checks to determine whether any chain of records and waiting programs will be closed by the latest request.

To resolve the deadlock, we need to free the resources held by one or both (or all) of the processes involved. The most drastic solution is to close down both programs, or even the entire system, and to restart in the hope that this deadlock will not recur. This is potentially expensive, but the frequency with which deadlocks occur may not justify anything more sophisticated. Sometimes, one of the programs can be compelled to release the resources it held with relatively little disturbance to the rest of the system. This is called *pre-emption*. When the program recognizes that its requests have been pre-empted, it may have to discard some partially completed work , and defer it until the resources it needs are available later. The amount of work involved depends on what the pre-empted program was doing at the time. Perhaps only a single transaction need be lost, but sometimes the program has to be aborted and restarted.

In some systems, deadlock is a regular and predictable occurrence which needs to be dealt with systematically by a pre-emption scheme of some kind. It may be quite expensive to implement, however. Many real-time application systems encounter deadlock only rarely, as a result of random coincidences of timing. One would not usually adopt pre-emption in such cases.

4.2 Duplication of hardware and data

A simple way to improve the reliability of a computer system is to duplicate the components which are likely to fail. The extra reliability to be gained can be calculated quite easily, and set against the cost of the extra equipment. This approach can be applied at any level, from standby telephone lines up to the duplication of complete central computer systems. How far one is prepared to go depends on the amount of money available and the value one sets on the reliability it buys. In extreme cases, such as defence or manned spaceflight systems, there may be three or four identical computers, each ready to take on the whole workload at a moment's notice.

More modestly, one might have:

- leased communications lines backed up by public switched network facilities;
- reserve terminals in some important offices;
- duplicated communications controllers or front-end processors;
- spare tape and disk drives, printers, card-readers, etc;
- twin central processors, spare channels.

The most expensive components are not necessarily the most critical. The failure of an operator console may stop the system just as effectively as the failure of the central processor worth perhaps 300 times as much

Using duplicate hardware

It is evidently wasteful to keep hardware sitting idle, waiting for a failure in the main system which may happen only rarely, and one would like to find some employment for the spare equipment during normal operation, when it is not required for back up. There are two possible approaches to this, which Yourdon (10) calls the *duplexed system* method and the *dual system* method.

In a duplexed arrangement, the primary system is capable of handling the full workload and runs on its own. The spare system is a complete copy of the primary system, and when required, it can take over all of its work. While the primary system is operating normally, the spare need not be idle, however. It can be handling a variety of jobs, such as :

- program development and testing, and other low priority batch work;
- file maintenance and re-organisation, general housekeeping for the primary system;
- file dumping and checking;
- off-line printing.

In a dual arrangement, the two halves of the system work in close co-operation with one another, normally sharing the processing load. The spare capacity can be used to meet unusual peak volumes of work, or to provide better response time or throughput. When one component fails, its twin immediately takes over the full load, although perhaps at reduced performance.

When very high standards of reliability and accuracy are required, two or more computers in a multiple system may each perform identical operations so that the results can be cross-checked between them. A logical extension of this is a *voting scheme*, in which three or more computers each perform the same task. The results are compared, and if only one differs from the verdict of the rest, it is presumed to be wrong and the majority is taken to be right. Such extravagant use of hardware is only justified in exceptional cases – once again, defence and spaceflight systems are possible examples.

Switchover

An advantage of dual systems is that they can react to the loss of one component almost instantly, and without noticeable interruption to service. One needs a hardware connection between the two processors and the logical capability in each control program to recognise whether or not the other half of the system is working properly. Each must be able to re-route the data previously entering the failed processor into itself, and to assume control of shared resources such as peripheral devices. Even then, the switchover process takes a finite, though perhaps very short, time during which input data may be lost. The complexity of the control software and the need for extra switching hardware ensure that the switchover process itself is not absolutely reliable, and one must take this into account in calculating the reliability of the combined system, as we shall see below.

Immediate switchover and uninterrupted service are luxuries which one cannot always afford. At the opposite extreme, the backup system may be no more than an arrangement with another company owning a similar

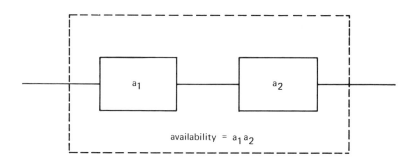

(a) Series connection

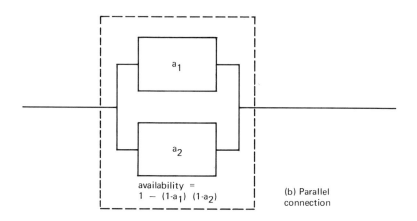

(b) Parallel connection

4.2   Combined components

computer configuration nearby. It may be several hours before the data files and the program libraries can be transferred to the backup machine, longer perhaps if other work is already running on it. This puts one at the mercy of another organization whose priorities and sense of urgency are quite different from one's own, a situation which few companies depending on a real-time service are prepared to accept.

In duplexed real-time systems, therefore, the backup system is usually on the same premises as the main computer. The program libraries will be available on both systems; all that is needed to change from one machine to another is to transfer the files, switch the communications lines through to the spare machine and to restart the system. If the peripheral devices on which the files are mounted can also be switched from one machine to the other, even the physical transport of data volumes can be eliminated. Switchover can be accomplished in a matter of minutes. This does not mean, however, that normal service can be restored immediately the failure of the main system may have caused some damage to the files which has to be repaired first.

Reliability calculations

The extra reliability gained by hardware duplication can be calculated quite simply, as outlined here and explored in more detail by Pritchard (11) and McGregor (12). We start from the *availability* of each of the major components of the system in question. The availability is defined (section 2.2) as:

(Mean Time Before Failure)/(MTBF + Mean Time To Repair)

McGregor gives some typical values for the availability of various components of a data-communications system; for example, 0.999 for a modem, 0.990 for a front-end processor, 0.997 for a telephone line. These are example values only, so they should be treated with some caution.

If two components are connected in series, the combined unit they form is available only if *both* component units are available. Suppose they have an availablity of a_1 and a_2 individually (a_1, $a_2 < 1$), then the combination has availability $a_1 a_2$ (*see* diagram 4.2a).

If two *alternative* components are connected in parallel (*see* diagram 4.2b), the composite unit is available if *either* of the single components is available. That is to say, it is out of action only if both the alternative components are. The availability of the combination is:

$(1 - (1 - a_1)(1 - a_2))$.

Diagram 4.3 shows an example. In 4.3(a) a terminal is connected to the computer centre by a leased telephone line with a modem at each end. The availability of the line and each modem is 0.99 and 0.997 respectively. The availability of the link from the terminal to the computer centre is:

$0.997 \times 0.990 \times 0.997 = 0.984$

4.3(b) shows the link including a backup line through the public switched network, directed through the same modems. This switched line has an availability of 0.97. The availability of the terminal-to-centre link is now:

$$0.997 \times (1 - 0.01 \times 0.03) \times 0.997 = 0.994$$

Exercise

What would the availability of the communications link be if the backup line were switched through separate modems, of the same type as those used on the leased line?

Calculations such as those shown above can be extended to much more complex cases. They are given here to illustrate the basic method, but also to point out some deficiences in it. The calculations implicitly assume that switching to the alternative unit is automatic, instantaneous and completely reliable. These conditions are rarely satisfied, if ever.

Allowing that the switching mechanism is reliable, let us consider the effect of switching time. The crucial factor is the ratio of switching time to MTTR. In the simple telephone line example given above, the operator may take several minutes to find out what was wrong, switch to the reserve line and dial through to the computer centre. This is very short by comparison with the day or so it may take to repair the leased line, so the availability calculation will only be slightly distorted.

If we tried to apply the same technique to calculate the availability of a duplexed computer system, the results could be meaningless. Let us suppose that the availability of a single computer system is 0.98. On the face of it, the availability of a duplexed system comprising two identical computers would be:

$$1 - (0.02 \times 0.02) = 0.9996$$

In fact, the availability given might represent about six twenty-minute interruptions in an average 100-hour working week. If it takes half an hour to switch the work from one machine to another, one would not usually bother unless the failure on the main system was of a kind likely to take a long time to repair. One would normally try to repair the fault on the main system and restart there without switching.

Duplicated files

Data files can be duplicated as well as hardware components. Two identical copies are kept and are updated in parallel; everytime a record is updated it must be written back to both files. The logic of this is handled by the data manager, and is invisible to the application programs. When one of the files or an individual record in it becomes unreadable, the data manager automatically switches to the duplicate file. The copy file can be used to repair or reproduce the original, either immediately or later when there is some spare time.

This technique is useful in protecting files against damage by hardware faults. It is not proof against faults in the application or supervisory programs, since incorrect records may be written in exactly the same way on both files. To get the full measure of protection, the main file and its copy should be located on different units and even on different I/O

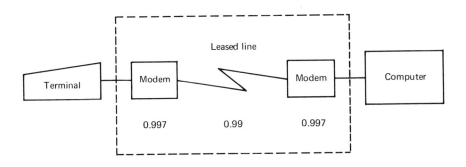

(a) Leased line only

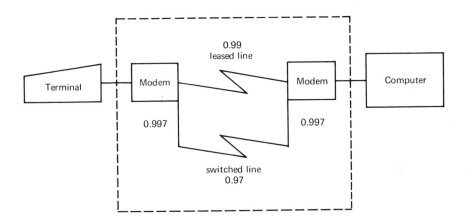

(b) Leased line and back-up switched line

4.3   Terminal-computer communications links

channels. This may prove expensive, as well as difficult to operate. Although file duplication uses extra devices and storage media and imposes an extra load on the devices and channels, it is interesting to note that it may actually speed up record retrieval from moving-arm disk units, as one can go for the copy of the record which is closest to its disk arm (Marsh, 2).

4.3 Graceful degradation

Computer systems, however well designed, are inevitably subject to faults. Some faults are more serious than others, and it would be a poor system which collapsed every time it encountered a minor hardware problem or an error in the database. We expect a system to adjust itself and carry on working whenever possible, giving up only when it is finally unavoidable. This process of adaptation is called *graceful degradation*. It involves:

– detecting and isolating the faults in the system so as to prevent further damage;
– continuing to work, perhaps providing a reduced service in a *fallback mode* of operation until repairs are completed.

In fact, repairs can be carried out sometimes while the system continues to run. Hardware units can be taken off-line while engineers work on them, or while they are subjected to test and diagnostic routines by programs independent of the main processing system. Faulty programs may be temporarily closed down while the maintenance programmers try to find out what is wrong with them, other programs continuing independently. Parts of the database may be isolated while the errors are found and corrected. Alternatively, repairs may be deferred until a time when the computer system can be closed down for more comprehensive tests and repairs

While the system continues to operate, it is unlikely to provide the same standard of service it normally does. It is said to *fall back* to an alternative mode of operation. This may simply mean a deterioration of performance following the loss of the full hardware capacity of the system. The same programs are competing for less main memory or disk, or fewer channels or processors, with a corresponding loss of throughput and response time. In other fallback modes, not all the normal facilities can be provided, for example:

– after a faulty program has been withdrawn, some types of transaction cannot be processed;
– transactions cannot be applied to records which contain errors or are stored on a faulty hardware unit;
– some facilities are withdrawn to allow the remainder to use a reduced hardware configuration;

  - some terminals get no service at all because of faults in the
    communications network.

Distributed intelligence

In each of the above, the central computer system is still largely intact
and is providing a restricted service which is presumed to be better than
nothing. Systems which contain some degree of distributed intelligence
can be designed to adapt even to the complete failure of the computer
centre. Data can be collected locally and saved until the centre is back in
service, then transmitted for processing. The data may be collected by
front-end processors which operate independently of the main system, or
at local concentrators or message-switching centres. They can also be
collected at the remote terminals themselves. In the past few years
terminals have become available which can support relatively cheap
storage devices such as miniature magnetic tapes, cassettes or 'floppy
disks'.

At a stage beyond this simple data collection facility, parts of the
database may be stored or copied at local centres, which also have a
processing capability of their own. If the central system or the links to it
fail, some types of work can still be processed locally, while those
transactions which cannot be handled are saved until contact with the
main centre is restored. Systems in which both intelligence and data
storage are distributed in many locations can clearly be made more
resilient to faults than those in which all the data and processing power
are concentrated in one computer. However, the problems and capabili-
ties of such systems have yet to be fully explored (13).

Database errors

The ability to absorb hardware failures is to some extent outside the
province of the individual system designer, since it depends on hardware
and operating system facilities over which he has little control. However,
there is much he can do to enable the system to accommodate errors in
the database. These vary from errors in single records caused by transient
faults, through the loss of groups of records such as tracks or cylinders,
up to the destruction of large areas of the database after a major hardware
failure. Provided the damage is not too extensive and the faulty areas can
be identified and isolated, the system may be able to continue processing.

This requires co-operation between the data manager and the application
programs which use the database. Any of these may detect an error. The
data manager may find parity errors or incorrect structural information,
or may not be able to read a record at all; the application program may
discover errors in the contents of the record and report them to the data
manager. The data manager is responsible for isolating the incorrect data
and initiating repairs, but they are nonetheless unavailable, if only

temporarily, and the application programs need to know what to do until the data they need are usable again.

On first finding an error in a retrieved record, the data manager should make a note of its location or key and lock it, that is to say, make it inaccessible. The application which originally asked for it and any other program which asks for it subsequently are notified that the record is not available. The data manager can now start a search program which attempts to access records in the vicinity of the erroneous one to find the extent of the errors. It may find that the error is an isolated one, or it may discover that a whole track or storage unit is faulty, and this enables a suitable plan for repairing the database to be worked out.

The subject of database repair is covered in the next two chapters. In theory, for some easily identifiable errors, the data manager might decide on a course of recovery action and initiate the repair programs itself. More usually, it would tell the console operator about the errors it had found and carry on as best it could, leaving decisions about the recovery strategy to the human supervisors of the system.

While repairs are in progress, certain areas of the database remain inaccessible to application programs. Some applications may be unable to do any work at all, while others may be able to process all but isolated transactions. In an order-processing system, for example, one may be able to deal with orders for anything except 16-gauge copper wire, for which the stock record happens to be damaged. The loss of the customer credit approval file, on the other hand, might mean that no new orders for more than $100 can be accepted. The loss of the sales statistics file may prevent the processing of some management enquiries, but not the acceptance of orders.

Suspended transactions

The transactions which cannot be processed may either be rejected completely, or they may be stored temporarily until something can be done about them. In the first case, a message is sent to the remote terminal operator who will then probably put the originating document – for example, a written order form – to one side, and will re-enter the transaction later. The second method may be no more sophisticated than writing the unprocessable transactions to a temporary disk queue until they can be applied. The nature of the application system sometimes requires a subtler approach, however, as the 'suspense account' system used in banking demonstrates.

In banking systems, it is undesirable to have sums of money floating about which do not belong to anybody and which cannot be applied to an account. Such unattached sums would upset the double-entry bookkeeping on which the accuracy of the whole system is based. Accordingly, *suspense accounts* are used to which transactions can be applied until they are identified and routed to the proper account. This idea can be used in computer accounting systems, particularly for transactions which cannot be applied because an account record is unavailable or in error.

A cheque drawn for £10 by Mr A, account no 123456, is paid in at his home branch, and a transaction to debit his account for £10 is entered at the terminal there. However, account no 123456 happens to be on a track of disk which is unreadable, so the debit for £10 is applied to the computer suspense account (say acccount no 000002). The suspense account has, in effect, settled Mr A's debt for him, and he now owes it £10. As soon as his account record has been repaired, a transaction will be processed to pay the suspense account £10 out of Mr A's account. In this way the books at the local branch balance, as the total amounts of entries transmitted through their terminals agree with the changes in their account balances and cash totals, and the transaction eventually gets to its proper destination.

Operating in a fallback mode is inevitably inefficient in some degree. The supervisory and application programs may find themselves spending a large proportion of their time avoiding erroneous records and diverting unprocessable transactions, and the work which is postponed must be processed sooner or later. Provided that the faults are not too extensive, that repairs can be completed in a reasonable time, and that an acceptable standard of service can be kept up meanwhile, fallback operation is workable. It is usually left to the operations staff on the spot to decide what 'extensive faults' or 'acceptable service' means. The supervisory programs can help by collecting statistics and reporting on the number of database errors encountered, the number of transactions which cannot be processed, and the average response time and throughput. There may come a time when fallback operation is no longer practical, and one is obliged to shut down the system completely and undertake immediate repairs.

4.4 Termination and recovery

Despite one's best efforts to prevent errors, and despite one's most ingenious attempts to carry on working with a partly-crippled computer system, on occasion there is no alternative but to stop processing, find and repair the faults, and start again. This may sometimes be a conscious decision on the part of the system operators; if continued processing is too inefficient or endangers the integrity of the database, they will tell the system to close itself down. More usually, one does not have this option. In the face of severe failures, there is little the supervisory programs can do to soften the blow, and the system will stop abruptly and without waiting for instructions.

Whenever possible, however, the supervisory programs should try to retain or regain control so that they can close the system in an orderly way. They will:

- finish any requests outstanding on the database, and make a note of any which could not be completed;
- force each application program to finish whatever it is doing and shut itself down;
- send a message to remote terminal operators warning them that the system is going off the air;
- make a record of the state of processing which can be used to reconstruct it later (a checkpoint – *see* chapter 5)
- make a record of any information which can help to find the cause of the system failure;
- finally, terminate themselves.

Ideally shutdown would take place completely under the control of the supervisory programs, and as much information as possible would be preserved for diagnosis and subsequent recovery. It is particularly important that the terminal users know what is going on, so that they can carry out any instructions they have for working without the computer. This ideal situation is not always realized, unfortunately.

When some or all of the programs in the system have been terminated, it is probable that some of the work that they have done up to that point is invalid or at least suspect, and has to be discarded. Part of the recovery process is undoing the effects of invalid processing to restore the database to a condition when the system is presumed to have been operating correctly. The discarded transactions have to be processed over again. It is wasteful to throw away more work than is necessary, and the more closely the effect of the failure, and therefore the recovery operation, can be confined, the better.

There are two aspects to the scope of the recovery operation – how much of the system has to be closed down, and over what period of time transactions have to be discarded. What we described above was a complete shutdown of the entire computer system. This is not always necessary; as we noted in 4.3 above, it is sometimes possible to close down a single program or a group of programs while the rest of the system continues in normal operation. However, by the time the error is discovered, incorrect results produced by the failed program may have been stored in the database and used by other programs. Only programs which are free from the suspicion of using incorrect data can be allowed to continue.

In a real-time system, there is an interdependence between programs established by the data they produce and use, which is very complex and constantly changing. It is, therefore, likely to be a difficult task to decide which programs are affected by a failure and which are not. The theoretical possibility has been discussed of keeping a dynamic record which can be used to untangle the relationships between the programs, and to decide which to terminate and how much of their work to reprocess (Davies, 14). At the time of writing, so far as the author knows, this work has not yet had any practical consequences. While such sophisticated and general methods are not yet available, interference between programs can be limited by cruder means by limiting their usage of the database. In 4.3 we showed how errors in the database may affect only certain programs or transaction types.

The other 'dimension' of recovery is the period of time over which work has to be discarded. We can limit this by establishing a record of the state of the system from time to time, at which we can assert with various degrees of conviction that the system is correct. These are the *dumps* and *checkpoints* discussed in the next chapter. By reverting to one of these correct states, we hope to be able to restart the system without any errors. What is more, by the use of special updating techniques (section 7.2), we may sometimes need only to recover the transactions current at the time of failure.

References

1. James Martin, *Security, accuracy and privacy in computer systems*, Prentice Hall, 1973.
2. S Marsh, *Error recovery in teleprocessing systems*, MSc thesis, Birkbeck College, University of London, 1973.
3. James Martin, *Systems analysis for data transmission*, Prentice Hall, 1972.
4. *System/370 principles of operation*, IBM manual No GA22-7000.
5. J K Iliffe, *Basic machine principles*, McDonald-Elsevier, 1968.
6. *B6700 system miscellanea*, Form No 5000367, Burroughs Corporation, 1974.
7. *Introduction to virtual storage*, IBM manual no GR20-4620.
8. James Martin, *Design of man-computer dialogues*, Prentice Hall, 1973.
9. J H Howard, *Mixed solutions for the deadlock problem*, Communications of the ACM, vol 16, no 7, July 1973.
10. E Yourdon, *Reliability of real-time systems*, Modern Data, May 1972 (part 5 of six parts).
11. J A T Pritchard, *Quantitative methods in on-line systems*, NCC Publications, 1976.
12. P McGregor, *Effective use of data-communications hardware*, National Computer Conference (US), 1974.
13. *Structures for future systems*, EDP Analyser, vol 12, no 8, August, 1974.
14. C T Davies, *Recovery semantics for a DB/DC system*, IBM Technical report TR02.528, May, 1972.

Chapter 5

Elements of a recovery system

5.1 Batch systems and file generation

Large scale direct-access storage systems are a relatively recent development. Only in the early 1960s did equipment become available which was capable of handling large files of data. Although magnetic disks and drums had been in use for some years before, they were of small capacity and suitable only for storing segments of program code and small data tables.

Business applications, and others needing to process large volumes of data, were obliged to use sequential storage media such as magnetic and paper tape and punched cards. Sequential processing has a long history and the techniques are very well understood. Even now, many applications still use sequential files updated in the batch mode. If there is no need for real-time response, the simplicity of this scheme makes it very attractive, and for suitable applications batch processing can be very efficient.

However, direct access devices make possible a variety of more sophisticated techniques for file storage and processing. In particular, they allow the files to be updated in place and this, as we noted in chapter 2, $\leftarrow$ complicates the integrity and recovery problem enormously. Before we go on to discuss this problem, we will look at the relatively simply recovery methods which are possible with file generation as they appear in a batch system. A warning is necessary here: batch systems, as described below, lend themselves very readily to file generation as a method of file backup and recovery, but they can and sometimes do use updating in place. The important distinction is between the update methods and the recovery techniques they entail; *not* between 'batch' and 'real-time'. Arguably, this terminology is already obsolete and will become less and less useful to describe systems based on the new generation of storage technologies, such as laser and electron-beam memories, which are under development at the time of writing.

Basic recovery scheme

In its simplest form, a batch system is based on a master file of records stored and accessed sequentially, in the order of a key such as an account number or product code. Transactions for updating the master file are collected into batches before they are processed. Before the update run they are validated and sorted into the same order as the master file, by the key of the record to which each transaction applies. Then they are processed against the master file in a single, sequential pass.

The master file is updated by reading a record from the old version, applying transactions to it if there are any, and writing an updated record to a new version of the master file. The new master file and the old are quite separate; the old file is unchanged and the new one is a fresh updated copy of it on a different reel of tape or disk pack. This is what makes recovery after a failure so simple. If anything goes wrong during the updating run, the old master and the sorted and validated transactions are still available to try again. Most tape drives have a facility whereby a tape cannot be overwritten unless a *write ring* has been inserted in the reel, and disk drives often have a switch which serves the same function. Thus, not even program or operating system failure can affect the file. The only way it is likely to be damaged, short of fire or flood, is by a mechanical failure which stretches or tears the tape, or scores the surface of the disk.

Successive versions of the files are often called *cycles* or *generations*. Recovery in batch systems is usually founded on the retention of previous versions of the master files, and the corresponding batches of input data. In the simplest system, three versions are used: the 'grandfather', the 'father' and the 'son'. Normally, transactions are processed against the father file to produce the son. If this goes through successfully, the son becomes the new father file, the father becomes the new grandfather, and the old grandfather file is discarded – that is to say, its tape or disk is released to be re-used.

Should the update run fail, the faults are corrected and the programs are run again to process the same transactions against the father file. If the father file itself is unusable, there is still a previous version, the grandfather, from which it can be reproduced. The *previous* batch of transactions are processed against the grandfather to recreate the father.

For additional security, one may keep more than three cycles of the master files. If only three cycles are kept in a daily processing system and an error is discovered four days after the fault which caused it, all the available versions of the files will contain the error. There is no way of correcting it, at least not by simple reruns. Evidently, cost and storage space impose practical limits to the number of cycles which can be kept, although six to ten is not unusual. There may be a number of master files occupying dozens or hundreds of volumes in total, and every extra cycle costs a significant amount in magnetic media and shelf space. In this respect, disk packs are more awkward than tape reels as they are bulkier, more fragile and much more expensive.

One must also consider the organisational problems of dealing with several different versions of the same files. Successive cycles are often distinguished from one another only by a single character or digit in the file name, or by the date of creation. It is vitally important that the right version is used. This requires good organisation in the library and the computer room, in issuing and returning volumes and mounting them on the right devices. It also demands software facilities to write and subsequently to check file labels (special identifying records at the beginning of each file or volume). Some operating systems provide facilities for naming and identifying cycles of a file automatically, for example *Generation Data Groups* in IBM's OS (1).

Multiple time cycles

So far we have supposed that files are updated on a single, fixed time-cycle – once a week, for example. In many systems, there is more than one updating cycle. Consider a personnel records system. The main employee file may be processed:

-   weekly, for amendments to addresses, sickness records, training details, transfers, etc
-   monthly, for regular personnel department reports
-   quarterly, for staff review and assessment, salary changes and promotions
-   yearly, for government statistical returns.

Different data items may be processed in each run, so that an error caused by a fault in the quarterly review program might not be noticed in the weekly and monthly runs, but would go undetected until three months later. Keeping several weekly versions of the file is no use for recovery, as they would all contain the same error.

The solution is to keep historical versions of the files for *each* of the time-cycles in which it is updated. One might keep four weekly files, three monthly files, four quarterly files, and possibly keep the end-of-year files indefinitely. Suppose that, at the quarterly review run in the Spring, it were discovered that the year end amendments had been applied incorrectly. The year end quarterly version of the file is still available; it can be updated properly with the corresponding transactions, to produce a file with the correct quarterly review fields, but in other respects three months out of date. An up-to-date version can be produced by substituting the appropriate fields into the latest weekly file.

Checkpoints and restarts

Resubmitting a complete update run, even if it is a sound method of recovery, may be an unnecessarily expensive one. Sometimes a run is interrupted by a minor hardware failure or by a transaction which was not validated properly. Although the programs cannot carry on until the fault has been corrected or the bad data removed, everything they have done up to the point of failure, or just before, is perfectly good. It would be wasteful to throw it all away and start again. This is especially true when the update runs for several hours. The MTBF of the system may be shorter than the average length of the run; if it had to start again from the beginning every time the system failed, the run might never finish at all.

In any job which takes more than a few minutes, there must be intermediate points from which the run can restart after a minor failure. It is usual to take *checkpoints* at intervals of five or ten minutes during the run. In their simplest form, these need contain only enough information to reposition the input and output files, and to restore balances, control totals and other relevant values in the update program. A checkpoint is a note of the state of processing which the program can use to reset itself and to carry on where it left off.

Checkpoints may be written on the output master file itself. When the system is restarted after the faults have been repaired, the update program reads the input and the output – old and new – master files in parallel until it reaches the end of the output tape.* Then it reads both files backwards until it reaches the first (ie, most recent) checkpoint, resets its totals, repositions the transaction file, and resumes processing. Any records after the checkpoint at the end of the output file are overwritten.

Alternatively, the checkpoints may be written to a separate file, perhaps a disk. Restart consists of reading the most recent checkpoint from the disk, repositioning the files and resetting the control values in the update program. Then normal processing is resumed, overwriting the end of the output new master file as before. The advantage of this latter method is that the files can be repositioned immediately, without searching for the end of the incomplete new master file.

All input and output files must be repositioned, not only the master files. The checkpoint must specify which transaction was last processed and how much printed output has been produced. Line printers obviously cannot be rewound like tape drives, so some output will probably be

---

* Locating the end-of-file is not always easy – see section 6.4

duplicated. The restart routine need only print a message to the computer operator telling him how much he should tear off and throw away.

In a simple batch system, checkpoints and restarts can be automatic functions of the operating system, at the request of a user program or as specified in job control cards. Several manufacturers provide software which will do this (2.3). However, since the software has no idea what data in the user program is relevant and what is not, it has no option but to dump the whole of the user's main storage space to the checkpoint file. Tailor-made routines can be more selective, so they are usually more efficient.

Intermediate types of system

The picture of batch systems presented above is necessarily a simple one. There are many approaches to systems design which fall between the classic batch update of a single master file and updating an on-line database in real time. On-line operation with remote terminals does not automatically imply real-time updating, nor even on-line master files.

A common approach is to collect and partially validate transactions from the terminal network during the day, to be processed overnight. When the network has closed, the transactions are sorted and validated to be processed in batches against the master files. The simple backup and recovery methods already described can be used to protect the master files; the data-collection files in which the transactions are stored are usually straightforward sequential data-sets which present no recovery problems. Regular checkpoints are taken during the day to limit the number of transactions which can be lost in a system failure. The only difficulty is in ensuring that none of the transactions received just before the failure are lost or entered twice; discussion of this is deferred to chapter 6.

When some degree of on-line updating is required, one may be able to compromise by keeping only a small part of the database on-line. In banking, a customer's account record contains much information which is of long-term interest only, such as balance statistics and accumulated interest and charges, none of which needs to be updated in real-time. It might, however, be useful to extract the account balances and put them in a separate, on-line file which can be updated whenever a transaction is posted to a customer's account, and which can be used to satisfy on-line enquiries. The extracted file will be much smaller than the original, and the scale of the recovery problem will be reduced accordingly.

5.2   Updating in place - an outline

As we explained in the previous section, recovery in file generation systems is based on reprocessing batches of transactions against the unchanged old master files. Failing that, one can use still earlier versions of the files and the corresponding batches of input data. When the files are updated on-line, this simple method is no longer adequate. Incoming transactions arrive in random order from a network of terminals and are applied immediately to the on-line files, overwriting the information that was there before. The concept of file cycles or generations is no longer of any use, as the files are changing continually.

There are, however, several points of similarity between batch and real-time systems. It is absolutely essential to keep copies of the files in some form to guard against a major disaster such as destruction of the computer centre by fire. This is equally important whatever method of updating is used. One is not so much concerned with such niceties as finding every error in the database or deciding exactly which transaction was the last to be processed; the vital necessity is to be able to produce a reasonably up-to-date copy of the files so that there is at least the foundation for recovery. In this respect, real-time systems are the same as batch systems, in that recovery is based on historical versions of the database kept in a safe place.

To this end, the on-line files are periodically copied onto a medium which can be taken away from the computer and stored, usually magnetic tape. This is called *file dumping* or *archiving*, and the copy is called a *file dump*. After a major failure, the database can be reconstructed by reloading the dump, and the system is then in essentially the same condition as when the dump was originally made. Many thousands of transactions received since then may have been lost, but this is better than no files at all.

It is only rarely that a failure destroys the files completely. Most faults which occur in everyday operation are less dramatic. They may cause minor damage to the database, but not enough to justify throwing it away and loading a dump in its place. We would prefer to keep most of the current database, repairing or replacing only those parts which are in error. This is, in fact, the major recovery decision to be made: whether to reload the files – which could take several hours – or to try to repair them as they stand after the failure. Which course one follows depends on the size and complexity of the files, the seriousness of the failure, and the urgency of the situation.

At any instant during normal operation, the database is likely to be in a highly volatile condition, with many transactions in progress and at various stages of completion. If processing is interrupted at an arbitrary point in time, the database will generally be in an inconsistent state which cannot be asociated with any particular transaction. Nor is it possible to determine how far each transaction had gone just by examining the database. Even after any known errors in it have been corrected, it cannot be used immediately to restart the system. To do that, one needs to know exactly which transactions have been processed, and one also needs full information about the processing state corresponding to the state of the database – for example, the values of control totals, positions of sequential files such as journals, and the contents of queues of outstanding work. Just as in batch systems, one must write *checkpoints* which allow the condition of the system to be reproduced during a restart.

Checkpoints are *static* pictures which record the state of processing at a fixed point in time. To restart using the information contained in a checkpoint, one must restore the database to the condition it was in at the corresponding time. Initially, one has either the database current at the time of the failure, or a version of it reloaded from a dump. To

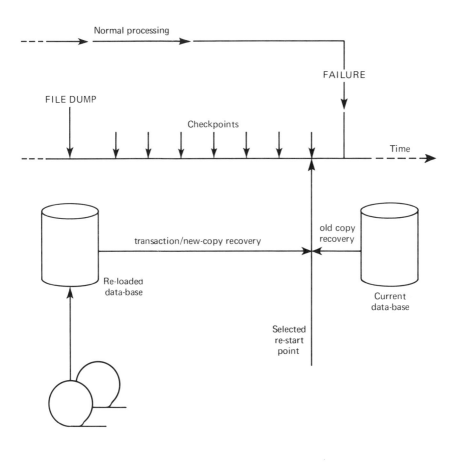

5.1   Alternative methods of recovery

reconstruct it as it was at any intermediate point, we need a *dynamic* record of everything that happened to it in between. Such a record is called a *log* or a *journal*.

One can store several different types of information on the journals. The most direct way of recording the activity of the system is to record all the incoming transactions as they are received. Changes to the database are caused by transactions. If one reloads the files as they were at time A, and reprocesses all the transactions which arrived between time A and a later time B, in their original order, one can recreate the files as they were at time B. There must be no partly-processed transactions in progress at time B; this must be ensured before a checkpoint is taken. One can use a transaction journal in this way, to restart after reloading the database from a dump. However, one cannot use it to process backwards from the current database to an earlier checkpoint. In general, a transaction is irreversible. If its effect is to add a value into a field in a record, it can be undone easily enough, but if it replaces information previously in the record – as when a name or address is amended – there is no way of knowing from the updated record and the transaction alone what was there before.

In reconstructing the database, we are interested in the final effects of the transactions rather than the intermediate processing. One can save unnecessary work by writing the database updates caused by the transactions on the journal, instead of the transactions themselves, and this provides an alternative method of reconstruction based on a dump. As we already observed, however, one does not always want to reload the database from a dump to recover from a minor failure. This may be acceptable for a small database; if it is sufficiently small, it can be dumped very frequently, perhaps with every checkpoint, so that one can reload it and reprocess subsequent work even for minor failures without incurring unreasonable overheads. This is clearly not a practical solution for a database of any size, however. One needs a different method, which allows one to start from the slightly damaged database as it was at the time of failure, and to reverse its state back to a prior checkpoint. To do this one keeps a copy of the *old* version of every updated database record. Then the system can be run in reverse by rewriting the old records to their original positions.

5.3 File dumping

Dumping is the process of copying the current version of all or part of a database from on-line storage to a medium, usually magnetic tape, which can be removed from the computer room and stored for safe-keeping. The main purpose is to create a backup copy of the database which can be used for reconstruction after a failure. A secondary purpose is often to carry out checks on the files or sections of files being dumped.

We are mainly interested in file dumping as a means of recovery. However, since a dump entails reading all the records in the database or in a sizable section of it, it is also a good opportunity to perform exhaustive checks on the data which would otherwise require a separate pass of the files. Martin (4) suggests a number of possibilities, amongst which are:

–   verifying cash balances and hash totals;
–   applying checks to individual records for validity or reasonableness;
–   collecting statistics on file activity;
–   extracting management reports and summary files.

In section 4.1 several more checks which can be applied to chain and pointer structures in the files were mentioned.

The simplest and most common method of dumping is to take a complete copy of the whole database, all at once. This is done when the system is otherwise inactive, so that there is a compact, consistent picture of the database frozen at a specific point in time. The usual pattern of activity in commercial real-time systems is that they are in service during normal business hours, but at night and at weekends they engage in other work – maintenance and housekeeping for the real-time system and miscellaneous batch-processing. These are suitable times for dumping the files.

Many applications demand twenty-four hour service, however, and do not allow such convenient breaks. Here are two examples:

–   police information systems; since criminals do not oblige by working regular business hours, neither can the police and their computers;
–   international air-line reservation systems; these have to accommodate different time zones over wide areas of the globe; in the middle of the night in a London computer centre, it is midmorning in Tokyo and late afternoon in Los Angeles.

In systems of this kind it is often not possible to stop work long enough to dump the entire database. In other cases, the sheer size of the database makes a complete dump impractical; 10 billion (10^{10}) bytes is by no means an exceptional size, and one or two examples can be found of databases of 100 billion (10^{11}) bytes or more.

How long does it take to dump files of this size? That depends, of course, on the performance of the available hardware. The IBM 3330 is, at the time of writing, typical of modern, high-speed, direct-access storage systems. The maximum data transfer rate to and from the disk is about 800 kilobytes/second (5). If one were to dump to the fastest available tape drives (6), which have a transfer rate of 1250 kb/second, the speed of the disk would be the limiting factor. In practice, the most efficient dumping programs take about five minutes to dump a 3330 pack, which is a speed of about 330 kilobytes/second. At this rate, it would take more than eight hours to dump a data base of 10 billion bytes. One could reduce this by running several dump programs in parallel, but the total channel capacity of the system would soon be saturated. For extra physical security, two copies of the dump are often required, which magnifies the problem still further.

It is unlikely that such a large database would be uniformly active, and substantial parts of it might not change at all in the course of a day's or a week's work. It would be wasteful to dump the inactive parts, even if it were possible. One may decide to dump particularly volatile files, or files which are critical to system operation, more frequently than the rest. It is often possible to divide the database into logically or physically independent sections which can be dumped on their own. Rather than dump the whole database at one time, one could dump, say, a seventh of it on each day of the week. Since there is no longer a single, contemporary dump of all the files, the recovery procedures are rather more complicated than before, though this, as we shall see in chapter 7 is not an insuperable problem.

To avoid closing the system down while it is in progress, the dump may be run as a multi-programmed job concurrently with the real-time work. A dump program makes heavy demands on the I/O capacity of the system, but one can usually prevent it from interfering with response times or transaction throughput by adjusting the processing priorities of the programs. There is also the likelihood that a real-time application program will want to access a record which is being dumped. The simplest way to handle this is to lock out a section of the database as it is dumped, so that some transactions may have to be deferred until the dump is finished.

The dump need not necessarily be organized on the tape in the same way that the original database is on direct-access storage; in fact, it may present a useful opportunity to re-organise the files. After a long period of on-line updating the efficiency of the system may deteriorate as the database is altered. Space is taken up by records deleted but not yet removed; the order of records is no longer the optimum for fast update and retrieval; files spill over into overflow areas and available space becomes fragmented and scattered. The files must be tidied-up at intervals to maintain performance at acceptable levels, and this may be done as part of the dumping process.

When the dump is arranged in a way substantially different from the layout of the database itself, it is said to be a *logical* dump. The alternative is a *physical* dump. In this case, the disks are read serially in the most efficient way possible, and are transferred onto the tapes in exactly the same order, without editing. This permits very high dumping speeds like those in the example above.

The dump organisation one chooses depends on the way in which one intends to use the dump for recovery. When reloading the entire database, speed is the main concern, and a physical dump can be reloaded at the same high speed at which it was written. A physical dump is also well suited to restoring a complete disk volume, or a file extending over several volumes, or any section of the database stored continuously and identifiable by a range of hardware addresses. To retrieve a single, small file or a particular group of logical records is a different problem, as they may be scattered over several volumes of the disk, and therefore dumped on several different reels of tape. Here one needs a logical dump organisation and also a directory which tells on which reel and where on the reel each file is to be found. This directory would normally be held on disk, and it would itself have to be dumped at intervals to tape.

As we have already noted, it is wasteful to dump the whole data base if only a small fraction of it has changed since the time of the last dump. If possible, one would prefer to dump only the parts which have changed. This is called *incremental* dumping or (7) *differential* dumping. The data must be divided up into a fairly large number of logically distinct sections – one may suppose that they are distinct files. At regular intervals, the incremental dump program checks the database and dumps only those files which have been altered since it was last run. A directory is needed to keep track of when each file was altered, when it was last dumped and where its most recent dump copy is to be found.

The problem with this method is that the dump is not a single, compact, well-organised affair but is scattered over a number of tapes in more or less random order. After a time, it may become quite difficult to locate the most recent dump of any particular file, and the tapes may contain many redundant, out-of-date dumps of very active areas of the database. Commonly, the incremental dump is backed up by a conventional complete dump taken at long intervals. In the meantime, the collection of incremental dump tapes is regularly re-organised and edited. They may be merged in with the complete dump, or simply purged of all of the superseded file copies. The directory specifies where the current copy of a file is to be found – in the main dump, the edited incremental dump, or a current incremental tape – so that it can be retrieved for recovery.

It is generally impractical to employ the incremental dump technique at the level of individual records; it is most useful when there is a large number of relatively small, independent files. It is widely used in time-sharing systems, which maintain files for many independent users. One of the best-known descriptions of file integrity in a university time-sharing system was published by A G Fraser of Cambridge University in 1969. The files were divided into user groups which would fit conveniently onto one reel of tape. The primary dump system was an incremental dump run approximately every twenty minutes.

On each occasion, it would dump the files updated in the previous twenty minutes to the current primary dump tape. These tapes were re-used, so that it was sometimes necessary to recopy a file whose current dump was about to be overwritten. The primary system was supported by a secondary dump system run as required, which maintained a distinct set of tapes for each group of users. Each time a secondary dump program was scheduled for a particular user group, it would update the previous dump tape cyclically, copying those files whose versions on the secondary tape were still valid and adding from the disk all those which had since been updated. The whole system was controlled by a file directory whose integrity was, of course, vital. For further details on this and on the methods of recovery used after failure, the original paper (8) is recommended.

5.4 Checkpoints.

A checkpoint is an image of the state of processing in a system at a fixed point in time; it allows that state to be reproduced in a subsequent recovery operation, should it be necessary. A checkpoint is a record of current working data normally held in main storage; it is associated with a particular state of the database which can also be reproduced, using the journals and file dumps. If the database is reconstructed as it was at the time the checkpoint was taken, the checkpoint itself can be used to restore the whole system to its original condition, from which it can be restarted.

Checkpoints are frequently used in rapid recovery from relatively minor failures. In this case, one wants to use the most recently available one to avoid unnecessary transaction reprocessing, and it should be readily available for use when required. Occasionally, a checkpoint other than the one most recently written will be used, if it is decided to restart from a particular time of day or if the latest checkpoint is incorrect or unreadable.

Several ways of storing the checkpoints are possible. They can be kept in a file of their own, written sequentially onto direct access storage. During recovery, the selected checkpoint can be quickly retrieved from the disk or drum and used to reset the state of the system almost immediately. Should the chosen checkpoint be incorrect, the one before it is used. Alternatively, the checkpoints may be written on one of the journal tapes, usually the old-copy journal. The advantage of this is that each is automatically associated with the corresponding state of the database, which is effectively defined by a position on the journal. However, one must then search the journal to find the required checkpoint. A compromise between the two methods can be achieved by writing the checkpoints to the journal, keeping also the latest one or two on direct access storage. There, they are easily accessible for use in a minor restart, while all the checkpoints are preserved on the journal in case of a major recovery operation and for use in diagnosis if need be.

The information to be stored in a checkpoint is a matter for the individual designer to decide, as it depends on the characteristics of the system. It may include some or all of the following:

- system and network configuration description; number, location and line addresses of signed-on terminals, status of local offices
- pointers into message queues by message type, terminal, priority, etc
- contents of in-core queues
- message sequence numbers from each terminal (for checking loss or double entry)
- current recovery information, eg journal file labels and record counts
- status of active programs
- allocation of system resources
- miscellaneous counts, totals, statistics
- current database information; space allocation, heads of chains, bad areas locked out, positions of sequential files
- status of temporary working files.

An effective, but sometimes inefficient, way to take the checkpoint is to dump the whole of the main storage space allocated to the supervisory programs, or even the whole of the machine's main store. Much of this is irrelevant to recovery, and it is better to be more selective. It is often the case that all the relevant control information is kept together in an inter-program communication area, so that it can be shared by the executive, the data-manager, the teleprocessing monitor, and any other program which needs it. The concentration of everything in a single data structure makes it easy to dump it as a checkpoint.

Checkpoints may be made on a variety of occasions:

- at specified time intervals, eg every ten minutes
- after a certain number of transactions, eg every time 5000 have been received since the last checkpoint
- when the processing load is light, to minimize interruption to service
- before critical points in the processing, eg before scheduling a file dump
- at the request of an application program
- at the request of the system console operator

- whenever the system is shut down
- to mark the successful completion of a recovery and restart operation.

It is useful also to take a checkpoint on starting a new volume of the old-copy or transaction journal. This will become clearer in chapter 6 but, briefly, if the system fails shortly after beginning a new reel of journal, the recovery program might have to read back to the previous volume before it can find a checkpoint, for which a full reel would have to be mounted, read to the end, rewound and taken down again. This can be avoided if a checkpoint is written immediately after a reel-change.

The checkpoint must reflect a stable, reproducible condition of the system and the database. Nothing must be in progress whose state is doubtful or which cannot be resumed in exactly the same place on restart. In particular, no partly-processed transactions or incomplete input/output operations should be outstanding. When the time comes for a checkpoint, the executive stops scheduling new programs and stops passing work to programs already in progress. Applications are allowed to finish the transaction they are currently working on, but are suspended as soon as they have completed it. The data-manager completes any outstanding operations on the database and the journals, checks that all programs are inactive, and writes the checkpoint records. If after an appreciable time there are still application requests outstanding which cannot be serviced, it is likely that two or more programs are involved in a deadlock. This is an error which must be resolved before the checkpoint can be taken, either by pre-emption or by closing the system down and restarting it.

As we have already noted, the complete picture of the system at any given time is composed of the database and the corresponding checkpoint. Some of the information required for recovery does not obviously belong in either; for example, temporary working files and transaction queues on disk. They can be regarded as part of the database; then they are dumped with it, and their activity is logged on the record journals. Alternatively, they can be treated as part of the current processing state, in which case they are copied at intervals, at the same time as a checkpoint or even as part of it. The working files may be highly volatile, so that logging changes to them on the journals would be a heavy overhead; on the other hand, they may be too large to dump frequently. The recovery technique must be decided according to the size and activity of the files in question.

5.5   Record and transaction journals

Journals are files (usually sequential) which provide a continuous historical record of the processing activity of a system. They have two main uses during recovery. First, they can be used in fault diagnosis, to discover the history of errors found in the database and their probable cause. Secondly, they can be used to correct the errors and to reconstruct the database so that the system can be restarted. There are other uses for journals which are not directly related to recovery and which do not concern us here; see, however, Martin (4) for further details. Journals are frequently also called *logs* or *audit trail tapes*.

Two broad kinds of information are written on the journals: incoming transactions and file-changes. They are, in a sense, equivalent. Transactions are processed by application programs and cause changes in the database. As the records are updated the alterations are noted on the file-change journals, and these are the final, physical consequences of the original transactions. This equivalence, and more specifically, exactly which changes correspond to which transactions, is of great importance in designing the recovery procedures.

The journals may actually be organised in a variety of ways, but it is useful to suppose that there are three, each being used in a different type of recovery.

1 The *transaction journal*. This holds a copy of each transaction, or each message containing transactions, which arrives from the communications network. The messages may sometimes be partially edited, and validated, and only the valid ones written on the journal.

2 The *old-copy journal* (OCJ), also called the before-image journal. This contains a copy of the old, unchanged version of any record or item in the database which is about to be updated.

3 The *new-copy journal* (NCJ), also called the after-image journal. This contains a copy of the new version of any record or item which has just been updated.

The methods of recovery allowed by each type of journal are described in the next chapter. Not every system needs to keep all three. There is an appreciable price to be paid for each, in processing and I/O overhead, and program complexity, and each is effective in dealing with certain classes of faults. The designer must decide which ones he wants to keep according to how susceptible his system is to various faults and how frequently they occur, and also according to how much he is prepared to pay for various standards of recovery performance.

Journal contents and organization

The simplest way to record file-changes, and the simplest to use during recovery, is to record the whole of a physical record whenever it is changed. This may be rather wasteful if one is only updating a single field in a record of several hundred characters, and far more information is logged than is strictly necessary. Certain data management systems allow individual items or fields of data to be accessed independently of their association as records, in which case the journals might contain individual items also. This will give a more compact journal, but not necessarily faster recovery.

The file-change journals (ie, the old- and new-copy journals) contain more than the simple image of the updated item or record. Information about its identity and origin is also needed. Associated with each entry in the journal might be:

- the file to which the record belongs, and its location within the file
- for a partial record, the location within the record of the updated field
- the identity of the program which updated it, or is about to do so
- the identity of the updating transaction
- the time that the entry was written on the journal.

There will be further information used during recovery to check that the journal was correctly written, eg:

- block numbers (to detect the loss of a complete journal block)
- block lengths
- the usual parity and block checks supplied by the hardware unit on which the journal is written.

The transaction journal may also contain extra data associated with each transaction recorded on it, eg:

- transaction sequence number
- the identity of the terminal from which it came
- the transaction type
- the program to which it will be routed
- the time at which it was received.

All this is available when the transaction has been received, identified and validated, but before it has actually been applied. A further entry may be made on the journal when the application program reports that it has been processed successfully.

During recovery, some dubious or incorrectly processed transactions are cancelled out by re-writing the old-copy journal entries to which they correspond back to the database. One must, therefore, be able to associate each transaction on the journal with the OCJ entries which it caused. A simple way to do this is to combine the OCJ and the transaction journal into a single sequential file, then the association is made by physical juxtaposition. Diagram 5.2a shows a combined transaction and old-copy journal and, in this case, how the checkpoints can also be written on the same file. The correspondence between old-copies and

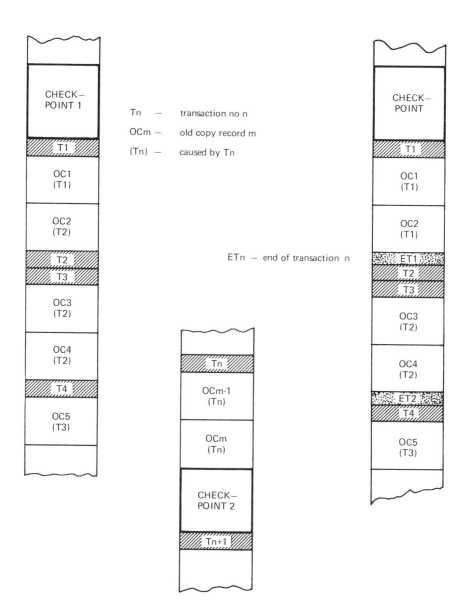

Tn   —   transaction no n

OCm —   old copy record m

(Tn) —   caused by Tn

ETn — end of transaction n

5.2   (a) Combined   trans-
       action and old-copy jour-
       nal   (b) Transaction end markers

transactions cannot be made at the individual level since there are usually several partly-processed transactions in progress at any given time, so that their entries on the journal are mixed up with one another. A checkpoint, however, represents a quiet time when no work is outstanding, so we can be sure that between any two of them, or between the most recent and the end of the journal, the old-copy records precisely correspond to the effects of the transactions. This is ensured by the rule that no updates may be made to the database until the old-copy data has been logged.

There is often no need during recovery to undo and reprocess any transactions other than those not complete at the time of the failure. If a note is made on the journal when a transaction is completed (diagram 5.2b), it can be ignored during a restart. Only those are reprocessed for which no completion marker can be found, and only the old-copy records associated with them are used to reset the database.

In some systems, all three journals are combined into a single file. This has the advantage of operational simplicity and reduces the number of tape or disk units tied up in writing journals. There are three possible disadvantages, however.

1 The combined volume of data written to the journal may overload the output device, so that logging becomes a serious bottleneck.

2 Not all the information on the journal is required during certain types of recovery – for instance, the new-copy records are irrelevant in a minor restart, which only uses transactions and old-copy records. Nevertheless, it all has to be read whether relevant or not, and restarts may take up to twice as long as they would if the NCJ and the OCJ were separate.

3 Most important, each journal provides a different means of recovery, and keeping them physically distinct provides a valuable safeguard against possible damage. A combined journal leaves one dangerously exposed, in that a single failure or accident could close all possible roads to recovery at once.

Volume calculations and operational problems

The volume of data which is written to the journals may be large. It is important to know how large, not only in deciding the organisation of the journals but also in assessing the operational problems and the effect on system performance. The following is an example of the type of calculation that is necessary.

Example

A large real-time system processes an average of 100,000 transactions per hour. Table 5.1 shows the characteristics of the three different types of transaction. Type 1 updates a single database record of length 800 characters. Type 2 updates a single type A record, and two type B records each of length 300 characters. Type 3 transactions are enquiries only and cause no alterations to the database. The information logged in an average hour is:

Transactions: type 1: 70,000 × 80 = 5,600,000
               type 2: 20,000 × 150 = 3,000,000
               type 3: 10,000 × 60 =   600,000
                                     9,200,000 characters

Old and new copies   A: 90,000 × 800 = 72,000,000
     (each)   B: 40,000 × 300 = 12,000,000
                                    84,000,000 characters

Assuming that all three journals are kept, the total volume of information logged would be more than 177 million characters an hour. Even using high density tapes and blocked journals, this system would generate several reels of journal tape per hour. The designer might think seriously about a method of storing only updated fields rather than complete records.

Type	Percentage	Length (chars)	Updates Type A	Type B
1	70	80	1	0
2	20	150	1	2
3	10	60	0	0

Table 5.1   Example transaction distribution

Exercise

Suppose that the transaction and old-copy journals are combined in a single file on the example system. The new-copy journal is kept separately. Both journals are written unblocked. Given that the data is written at a density of 6000 characters per inch and that there is an inter-record gap of one inch, how many feet of each journal are written in an average hour? How many standard 2400 ft reels is this in a twelve-hour working day? What if the two journals were written in blocks of average size 8000 characters?

Although the example describes an imaginary and very large system, more modest systems may still produce a dozen or more reels of journal tape a day, especially if high-density tape drives are not available. The journals must be kept for several days at least, to guard against the delayed appearance of errors. A large number of volumes are tied up in old journal. For cost reasons, magnetic tape is usually chosen as the storage medium, though there is nothing to prevent the use of removable disk packs.

Since the real-time system cannot operate without the journals, it is important that the change to a new reel when the previous one is full be made as quickly as possible. The new reel should already be mounted on the drive and ready for use when the journal writing program asks for it. The program can help the system operators to anticipate the change if it keeps a running estimate of how many feet of tape it has used. A few minutes before the next reel is actually needed, it will print a warning message, and the operator can then put the new reel up on a spare tape-drive.

Journal accumulation

The journal has to be retained at least as far back as the last file-dump, and if dumps are taken infrequently, the journal can grow to dozens of volumes. It is then very cumbersome to use for database reconstruction, when one needs to reload the whole database and read through the whole journal from beginning to end. The journal does, however, contain a good deal of redundant information, as some records may have been updated many times since the dump. Only the most recent new-copy version is relevant to reconstruction.

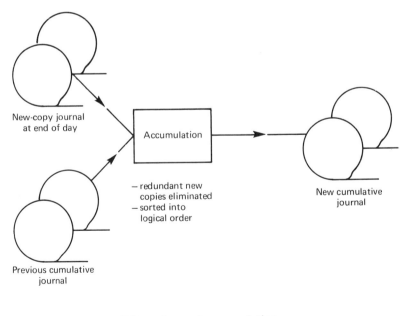

5.3   Journal accumulation

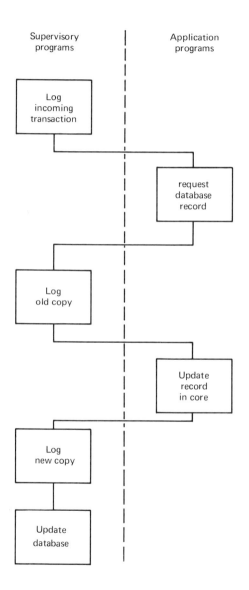

5.4   Logging and updating cycle

One can edit out all the surplus, superseded new-copies to obtain a journal which is logically the same as the original and just as good for database reconstruction, but more compact. This is done by running an editing program at intervals – say, at the end of every day – to add the changes for that day into a cumulative journal, discarding duplicates and retaining only the most recent version of each record (diagram 5.3). The database can then be reconstructed using the cumulative journal to the beginning of the day, followed by the current day's new-copy journal up to the point of failure. The accumulation program can also be used to sort the updates in the cumulative journal by file and record key, or into any other order which is convenient for recovery. Since there are no longer any duplications, there is no need to preserve the time sequence of the original journal. IBM's IMS data management system uses a log accumulation technique (9).

Journal writing and termination

At the time of a failure the journal writing routines, like all other processing in the system, is interrupted at an arbitrary point, perhaps in the middle of writing a record to the tape. It is most important that no changes be made to the database before the old copy of the data has been written successfully to the journal, otherwise a well-timed failure might cause an incorrect update which cannot be put right. What if we write the journal old-copy of the record first, and the system fails before the database is changed? The worst that can happen during a restart is that the surplus old-copy record is used to reset the database unnecessarily, but no harm is done. The basic cycle for updating the journals and the database is shown in diagram 5.4.

It is often asserted that journal tapes must always be unblocked and unbuffered. Otherwise, it is argued, there may be some journal records still in main store and waiting to be written out at the time of the failure. Authors who maintain this view go on to say that it is essential that the log tape be correctly terminated, or the integrity of the data-base is threatened. What they do not recognise is that *it is never possible to guarantee the correct termination of the journals and any recovery technique which relies on it is, in some circumstances, bound to fail.*

The restart method described in section 6, which uses the old-copy and transaction journals, does *not* depend on this requirement. For complete safety, any major database reconstruction should be followed by a restart of this type. It requires only that the old-copy journal record is written before the database is updated. This is easiest to achieve with unblocked and unbuffered journal files, but it is possible even when blocking and buffering are employed. A simple check-list should be kept in main storage of those journal records which have been put into a buffer but not yet physically written, so that no database update is allowed until confirmation is received that the block containing the old-copy entry has actually been transferred to the tape. Standard access methods may not always provide an easy method of doing this, so some minor modifications to the software may be necessary. On the other hand, the example above showed that an unblocked log may be unacceptable in a large system; it may affect throughput disastrously, or use up tape so fast that the system is impossible to operate.

Those systems which do rely on correct log termination generally use a special log terminator program which is run immediately after the failure. It finds the region of storage in which the system was running, traces pointers and control blocks to find any buffers and partially-complete blocks waiting to be written out, and transfers them onto the journal tape. However ingenious the program, there are several circumstances under which this will not work, for example:

- – a software fault has destroyed the information the log terminator needs to find the buffers;
- – the unit on which the journal itself was being written failed, in such a way that several blocks of journal data are incorrect and cannot be reproduced from the contents of the buffers;
- – the contents of main storage were lost during the failure.

The last is an acute problem with some modern computers which use semiconductor main storage, the contents of which will not survive a power failure.

References

1. *OS/360 Job Control Language Reference*, Appendix D, IBM manual no GC28-6704.
2. *Advanced Checkpoint/Restart*, IBM manual no GC28-6708.
3. *A narrative description of the B5500 Disk File Master Control Program*, Burroughs Corporation, 1966.
4. James Martin, *Security, Accuracy and Privacy in Computer Systems*, Prentice-Hall, 1973.
5. *3830 Storage Control and 3330 Disk Storage*, IBM manual no GA26-1592.
6. *3803/3420 Magnetic Tape Subsystem*, IBM manual no GA32-0020.
7. E Yourdon, *Reliability of Real-Time Systems*, Modern Data, June 1972 (part 6 of six parts).
8. A G Fraser, *Integrity of a Mass-storage Filing System*, Computer Journal, vol 12, no 1, June 1969.
9. *IMS/360 Utilities*, IBM manual no SH20-0915.

Chapter 6

Recovery techniques for real-time systems

6.1 Preparation for recovery

Let us summarize the steps in the recovery process from the initial failure to the final restoration of normal service:

- the fact that the system has failed is recognized
- the type of failure is determined
- the faults in the system which caused the failure are identified
- the extent of the damage is determined, in the database, programs, system files and elsewhere
- a method of recovery is selected
- faulty programs and hardware units are repaired
- the database is repaired or reloaded, as appropriate
- restart programs are run which reset the state of the system, undo and reprocess any incorrectly applied transactions, and re-open contact with the terminal network
- normal processing is resumed.

We have already discussed faults and failures and the process of diagnosis, part intuitive, part logical, by which one finds the connection between them. The knowledge of why a failure happened is not always enough to enable one to decide how to recover. A transient fault may occur only once, corrupting a single record or item or only a single bit of data. On the other hand, it may have been happening intermittently for some time and there may be many other errors in the database besides the one which actually causes a failure. If these errors are not found and corrected, the system may fail again very soon after it has been restarted.

To avoid the risk of wasting a good deal of time and causing even more damage, it is wise to run a series of check programs on the database, to find all the errors before attempting a restart. These may be the same programs which are run at regular intervals as a routine check; adding up hash totals and balances, verifying record chains and lists and comparing copies of duplicated files. However, one does not often have the time to do a comprehensive check on the whole database. In diagnosing the faults, one should get some more specific idea of where to look for further errors. It is useful to have programs which check or print out for visual inspection subsets of the database, such as:

- all records in a particular file
- all records within a specified range of keys
- all records updated by a particular program
- all records stored on a given unit, or a set of cylinders or tracks of a particular unit
- all records updated in a specified time interval
- all records included in a given chain or list
- all records updated by a particular transaction or type of transaction
- all records updated from a particular terminal.

The conditions may be combined. One might want, for example, a print of all records altered by terminal 22B4 since 10am. To check the file selectively, the information on which the selection is made must be stored, either in the updated records themselves or on the journal tape. The journals can be scanned to produce a list of suspect records, which are retrieved from the database and checked for correct updating.

When the database has been examined as thoroughly as time allows, one should be able to decide how to go about repairing it, and to estimate how long the repairs are likely to take. One needs to know:

- which individual records must be corrected or replaced
- which areas of the database must be completely reloaded
- how old the errors are
- where (in the file dumps or journals) the correct data can be found
- which transactions have to be reversed and processed again.

There are three basic methods of recovery to choose from, each of which is described in more detail in the sections which follow. For minor failures – that is to say, those which leave the database largely intact – there is a method which uses the old-copy journal and transaction log to reverse the effects of recent trransactions and to process them afresh. More serious failures require that the database be reloaded from a dump, and the new-copy journal is used to reproduce the subsequent updates. Finally, one may reload a database dump and reprocess all subsequent work using the transaction log.

With certain kinds of fault, one method of recovery or another is immediately ruled out. Program faults for example, cannot be corrected using the new-copy journals, since they contain the incorrect updates made by the faulty program. The faults must be rectified and the transactions applied again. Even when more than one method of recovery is feasible, they may not be equally practical. If the database were full of errors which had accumulated over a period of days, one might chose to do an old-copy journal restart, running back further and further until the oldest error was eliminated; it would often be quicker, however, to reload the most recent correct database dump and to use one of the other techniques.

Ideally, one would like to be able to leave file reconstruction to a standard procedure which, once set in motion, would require no intervention until the system were restarted. It would locate all the recovery information it needed in the file dumps and journals and would automatically reload or repair the files. In practice, few recovery systems are as sophisticated as this, and they might prove hopelessly inefficient if they were. If one knows that there are only one or two isolated errors to be corrected, and what the corrections should be, one may choose instead to use a special 'fix program', which alters the files directly, substituting information keyed in or punched on cards for that in the incorrect records. In an emergency, a maintenance programmer may even write an ad-hoc program to correct a single error.

There are obvious dangers in one-off fix programs. There is no opportunity to test them properly, and they may cause more damage than they correct. All the usual data validation checks are ignored, so that the substituted information may itself be incorrect. What is worse, they give the maintenance or operations staff an uncontrolled method of altering data which may be valuable or confidential. Since file fixes are sometimes unavoidable, it is better to provide a properly tested fix program which validates the corrections and keeps a log of both the old and the new versions of the altered data, together with the time and the identity of the program user, and any other relevant details. At least this is required for satisfactory auditing and security. The program may be restricted to holders of a security password, and the log should record both successful, authorized uses of the program and unauthorized attempts.

Similar security problems arise with emergency corrections to programs. Diagnosis may reveal a program fault which has to be corrected before recovery can begin, and the urgency of the situation makes the regular procedures for program alterations impractical. Once again, there is no chance to test the amendment properly, and there is a risk of introducing new errors, besides the possibility of deliberate breaches of security. The problem may be partly solved by applying all emergency changes through an editing program which keeps a log of the old and new source code and, like the file fix program, checks the authority of the programmer using it. As always, however, one is obliged to put some faith in the competence and honesty of the staff on the spot.

6.2   Recovery using the old-copy journal

The old-copy journal allows a relatively fast and simple method of recovery after a minor system failure. The essential condition is that the database should still be in a usable state. Many types of failure leave it largely untouched. A power failure, for example, should not of itself affect the files; the only errors likely to be introduced are the inconsistent updates left behind by programs interrupted by the breakdown. Other failures may cause only a few isolated errors which can easily be found and rectified without reloading the database.

Basic method

The object of the old-copy journal restart is to reverse the effects of the interrupted transactions and any others which have been applied incorrectly, to drive the system back to a point where it was free of errors, and to resume processing from there. It proceeds as follows:

1 The volume of the journal current at the time of the failure is mounted, if it is not already up, and is positioned after the last record written.

2 The journal is read *in reverse* – towards the beginning of the tape – restoring the old copy records to their original addresses in the database. Thus, more recent versions are overwritten by earlier ones as the tape is read backwards.

3 This continues until a checkpoint is reached. It may be the first one encountered (most recently written), or one designated by the operator. He may select the last checkpoint written before 3pm, for example, or the last before program X was started.

4 The checkpoint records are checked to make sure they are valid, and are used to restore the processing system's control tables. If the checkpoint contains errors, the restart continues back to the previous one, rewriting old-copy records as it goes.

5 When a good checkpoint has been found and loaded, the journal is read *forwards* again to position it after the last valid record written. It is then ready for use by normal processing programs as soon as the restart is over.

6 All transactions received after the checkpoint have been reversed, and must be processed again. They are collected from the transaction log, and re-queued. If a combined old-copy journal and transaction log of the kind described in 5.4 is used, the transactions are picked off as the journal is read forwards in stage 5.

7 A checkpoint is written to indicate that the restart is complete. Application programs are started and, as soon as the backlog of transactions is sufficiently reduced, contact with the terminal network is restored and normal processing resumes.

Shortened version

In the method described above, the section of the journal which represents the time between the selected checkpoint and the failure is preserved. There is one school of thought which maintains that this is necessary to keep a complete record of what the system has been doing, for future diagnosis or to allow the same restart to be repeated if need be. An alternative view is that, once the restart is finished, this section of tape describes a period in the history of the database which has been completely effaced, so the tape itself can be overwritten. In this case, one can speed up the restart by eliminating stage 5, and also save some space on the journal.

There is no more to be done if the transactions are logged on a separate file, but if they are kept in a combined old-copy and transaction journal then they, too, will be overwritten in the shortened restart. They must be saved in case they are needed in a future recovery attempt. The procedure can be modified as follows:

2a As the journal is read backwards, the transactions are picked off and written into a temporary work file.

5a A fresh checkpoint is written to mark the completion of the first phase of the restart.

6a The transactions are retrieved from their temporary file in the *reverse* order to that in which they were written in stage 2a – that is to say, in the order in which they were originally received from the terminals. As they are fed to the applications programs, they are logged again.

In practice, this shortened form of old-copy restart can be notably quicker than the more conventional method. One must take a good deal of care, however, that no essential information is destroyed that would prevent future restart attempts. In particular, the consequences of another failure interrupting the restart before it is finished must be considered. In phase 6a, for example, we are already irrevocably committed to overwriting the end section of the journal, which will be of no use to us if the restart now fails. What would happen if there were a read error on the temporary transaction file? It is as well to keep this file in duplicate, perhaps one copy on disk and a back-up on tape.

So far, we have assumed the journals to be the primary source for transactions to be reprocessed in the restart. This is not always necessary; there may be some more convenient source. In many systems, the raw transactions received from the terminals may be validated and partly processed before they are passed on to the application programs, and this intermediate form can be used to save some work during recovery. Suppose that the incoming transactions are preprocessed by the supervisory programs and added to queues on disk. These queues are not overwitten, but grow progressively during a day's work. As the new transactions are added to the rear of the queue, the applications (under the control of the executive program) read and process those at the front.

We can use this transaction queue to simplify the restart procedure considerably. During stage 2 – reading backwards to the checkpoint – transactions are ignored completely. When the checkpoint is reached, it is used to reset the pointers indicating the current positions at which the applications are working on the queue. The pointer to the rear of the queue, however, is *not* reset, since the preprocessed transactions are still usable.

Selective transaction reprocessing

In all the variations we have described so far, recovery with the old-copy journal is quite indiscriminate in that it eliminates all updates between the failure and the specified checkpoint. This may sometimes be rather wasteful. One may, for example, know that the only transactions which need be eliminated are those interrupted and incomplete at the time of the failure; or one may know that the errors are due to one particular program, and the work processed by other programs is still valid.

How can one determine whether or not a transaction is complete? One needs to provide some mechanism for an application program to tell the data-manager that it has finished processing a transaction, so that the data-manager can write a special marker record on the journal. Equally important, one needs to associate each old-copy record with a particular transaction so that only the incomplete updates are reversed. This may be done by marking each old-copy with the identifying number of the transaction which updated it. With these provisions, we can modify the basic recovery technique to ignore all completed transactions. The implementation presents some minor difficulties, but there follows a sketch of how it might be done, assuming a combined old-copy journal and transaction log.

During stage 2 of recovery, two lists should be kept:

A   A list of all transactions whose end-markers have been found, but not the corresponding transaction itself.

B   A list of all incomplete transactions, where the transaction or an old-copy record related to it has been found, but not the end marker.

As the journal is read backwards, each record read is an end-marker, an old-copy or a transaction.

- if it is an end marker the identifying number is added to list A
- if it is an old-copy and the transaction identity corresponds with one in list A, it is ignored. Otherwise, it is written back to the database and this transaction identity is added to list B
- if it is a transaction, and it is already noted in list A, the entry in list A is deleted. Otherwise, it is entered in list B

At the end of stage 2, list B notes all the incomplete transactions, which are re-applied during stage 6. There are some weaknesses in the method outlined – the reader is invited to consider, for example, why list A should be empty when a checkpoint is reached, and what he would do if it were not.

Supposing that one had identified a particular program as the cause of failure and the source of all errors in the database, one might want to restrict the recovery so that it reversed only the effects of the faulty program. Again, the basic information must be stored on the journals. Each transaction and each old-copy record must be marked with the identity of the program responsible, so that only these are selected in stages 2 and 6 of the recovery procedure.

This is easily done so long as the records updated by the faulty program have not subsequently been used by any other program. Sometimes, the program may process its own, exclusive files to which no other program has access, but the general case is more difficult. Programs may read the faulty data without updating it, so that there is not even a record on the journal tape. In a real-time system, the dependence of programs on data produced by other programs is complex and changing constantly. Some theoretical work has been done on the subject – see Davies (1), for example – but in practice it is difficult to implement a scheme of individual program recovery except in special cases.

Journal on direct-access storage

The old-copy journal is a sequential file which hitherto we have assumed to be stored on a sequential medium such as magnetic tape. There may be advantages in keeping at least part of it on direct access storage, however. One might, for example, retain the tape journal but keep a copy on disk of the section since the most recent checkpoint. Every time a new check-point is taken, the temporary disk journal is overwritten. At some installations, the disk units have a higher data transfer rate than magnetic tape, and this in itself speeds recovery from minor failures. The direct access facility allows the journal to be 're-positioned' without reading through all the intervening records, and this saves time at stage 5 of the basic recovery method. There are more advantages in the modified method in which only incomplete transactions are processed. During stage 2, the disk address of incomplete transactions is noted as well as their identity, so that they can be retrieved directly for reprocessing.

Calculating restart times

Provided that the database is in sufficiently good repair after a failure, the old-copy journal restart and its variations can be a rapid and effective means of recovery. This section is concluded with a simple calculation to find the average restart time using the basic method. The example system of section 5.5 is used.

The old-copy and transaction journals are combined into a single log which is written, unblocked, on magnetic tape. The database is stored on three disk packs. The characteristics of the hardware are as follows:

Magnetic tape units

> Tape speed: 200 inches/sec
> Recording density: 6000 char/inch
> Transfer rate: 1.2 million char/sec
> Start/stop time: 10 ms

Disk drives

> Transfer rate: 800,000 char/sec
> Rotation time: 16 ms
> Average rotational delay: 8 ms
> Average seek time: 25 ms

Checkpoints are taken every six minutes. If the system fails just before a checkpoint, nearly six minutes of work has to be processed during recovery, but the average is only three minutes. In three minutes, the following is written to the journal:

> 3500 type 1 transactions (80 char)
> 1000 type 2 transactions (150 char)
>   500 type 3 transactions (60 char)
> 4500 type A records (800 char)
> 2000 type B records (300 char)

There are 11,500 records totalling 4,660,000 characters of data. We assume that the journal is still positioned at the end-of-file after failure, and has not been rewound. To read backwards to the previous checkpoint takes:

> data transfer time $= 4,660,000/1,200,000 = 3.9$ sec
> $+$ start/stop time $= 11,500 \times 0.01 = 115$ sec
> total time $= 119$ seconds.

However, as the old copy records are read from the tape they must be written to their correct place in the database. There are 6,500 records to be re-written, total length 4,200,000 characters. The total input-output time is:

$$(4,200,000/800,000) + 6,500 \times (0.025 + 0.008) = 220 \text{ seconds.}$$

This would be close to the actual time taken if the records were all written on the same disk unit. The database is stored on three units, each capable of handling a write operation independently and in parallel with the others. If we assume that the records are distributed evenly over the three units, the I/O time on each is about 73 seconds. The disk writing, therefore, is largely overlapped by the tape reading, which takes slightly less than two minutes.

When the checkpoint is reached, it is used to restore the system's control tables. This should take no more than a second or two. Then the tape is read forwards again, and the transactions are reprocessed. Updating the database should take approximately the same time as resetting it with the old-copy records, and is again taken to be overlapped by the time to read the journal, which is approximately two minutes, as before.

Assuming, as we have done, that the system fails half way between checkpoints, the restart takes about four minutes. In the worst case, with a failure shortly before a checkpoint was due to be taken, the restart time would be eight minutes.

There are some obvious deficiencies in the calculations above, which make them useful only as a rough guide. The channel capacity is not considered, nor is the distribution of the files on the disk units, and the input/output times are overlapped in a very crude way. The read-time for the tape is calculated on the assumption that the tape stops and starts again between each record, which may not always be so. More accurate results could be obtained from a simulation model of the recovery system, provided that it was sufficiently detailed.

Exercise

The unblocked journal tape is seen to be a possible bottleneck in the performance of the system. Suppose further that it is unbuffered; each write operation has to be completed before the next can be initiated, so the tape must stop and start between each record written.

a) What limit does the *journal* impose on the volume of trans-actions the system can handle? Assume the same distribution of transactions as in the example.

b) Suppose the journal is written in blocks of average length 8000 characters. What is the average number of blocks written between checkpoints, assuming the same transaction processing activity as in the example? How long does it take to read them, assuming the tape stops and starts between each block? What is

now the limiting factor on the speed of the restart? How long
does it take, on average?

6.3 Database reconstruction

Two methods of recovery are available if the database is too badly
damaged by a failure to be usable in a restart. The basis for either is a
database reloaded from a previous dump. A dump, however, represents
the state of processing at some past time, perhaps many hours or days
before the failure. All the work done since then is lost; it may be
recovered either by using the new-copy journal or by reprocessing all
transactions received since the time of the dump.

Recovery with new-copy journal

This method proceeds as follows:

- the database is reloaded from an error-free dump
- the new-copy journal commencing at the time of the dump is
  mounted
- the journal is read forwards. Each new-copy record is written
  back to the database in the position to which it belongs, as
  specified by the control information associated with it on the
  journal.

This may continue while many reels of journal tape are read. The
recovery can be completed in a number of ways. One can carry on
reading and restoring records until the end of the journal is reached and,
in some cases, resume normal processing immediately. To do this,
however, one must be able to guarantee that the reconstructed database is
in a consistent state. The failure might have interupted the processing of
several transactions. Provided the contents of main memory has been
preserved, one may run a termination program immediately after the
failure which will write any outstanding records onto the end of the
journal and which will find out exactly what stage each transaction has
reached. The journal can then be used to bring the database fully
up-to-date, and the interrupted transactions can be completed.

This procedure is useful only in a limited number of cases, as it requires
intact the contents of main memory and the ability to resume a transaction in the middle of processing. Recovery can be rounded off more
safely with a restart of the kind described in the previous section. Any
partly processed or doubtful transactions are eliminated, and the consistency of the database is ensured. Alternatively, one can disregard the
doubtful tail-end of the journal completely, and stop restoring new copies
at the place corresponding to the last valid checkpoint. The remaining
new copy records are ignored, and all transactions received after the
checkpoint must be reprocessed.

The latter method presents a minor difficulty in deciding where to stop reading the journal. If the checkpoints are written in a separate file of their own, it is easy to read the most recent, validate it, and identify the corresponding position on the journal. When they are written on the old-copy journal, however, it must be read from the end backwards until a valid checkpoint is found and must be repositioned at the end before normal processing is resumed. Keeping the last checkpoint and the following section of old-copy journal on direct-access storage is very useful here, as the required checkpoint can be retrieved immediately.

Recovery with transaction journal

In this case, recovery proceeds as follows:

– as above, the database is completely reloaded from a dump taken before the failure and known to be error-free

– the transaction journal is mounted, beginning with the volume current at the time of the dump

– the journal is read forwards to the end and all transactions received after the dump are re-queued and reprocessed, in the same order in which they first arrived. Those which do not alter the database – enquiries – may be ignored, unless there is any reason to suppose that the responses originally sent were wrong.

– when all the transactions have been re-processed, or when the queues have been reduced to a manageable size, the terminal network is opened for normal business.

It is important that no transaction be lost or processed twice during recovery. Each is asociated with a transmission number assigned consecutively, so that gaps in the sequence, duplicates, or out-of-order transactions can be detected. The way in which this is used to communicate with the terminal operator is discussed in 6.5. In recovery with the transaction journal, the numbers provide a check on the continuity of the journal tape. Any gaps can be filled in by asking the operators to re-enter the missing transactions. The transaction after the last one recovered from the journal should be the first to be re-entered.

A disastrous failure such as a fire at the computer centre may well destroy the record and transaction journals as well as the database. Copies of the file dumps should always be taken away from the centre and stored in a physically secure place as soon as possible. The journals, however, are produced continuously and would not normally be removed and stored until the end of a day's work. There is a significant and unavoidable risk that all normal means of recovery might be lost in a major accident. In this event, the only solution is to key the transactions in again from the remote terminals, perhaps using the local hard-copy output as a source.

Comparison

The basis of either method of recovery described above is reloading the whole on-line database, which may take many hours. As we shall see in chapter 7, there are elaborations of the basic techniques which reload and reconstruct only those areas which are damaged. The new-copy journal technique is easier to adapt, since the journal can be organized in a way closely related to the physical layout of the database. Records on the tape could be identified, for example, by the disk unit and address of the database record to which each corresponds. One could then design the recovery procedures to reload single disk packs, or even single tracks or cylinders. Transactions, however, refer to logical records which may physically be scattered over several storage units. It may be possible to isolate logical files which need to be reloaded and to reprocess only those transactions which update them, but this would usually be less efficient than reloading physical storage areas.

Even after reloading the database, or the relevant parts of it, reading the journals and reconstructing the relevant areas may take a considerable time. The older the dump used, the longer is the journal which has to be processed. Reprocessing using the transaction journal involves:

- reading each transaction from the log
- retrieving the records to be updated from the database, including index and list searches, etc
- retrieving records from reference files, if any
- processing the data
- writing the records back again.

Reprocessing using the new-copy journal, however, involves only:

- reading each record from the journal
- writing it directly back to where it belongs.

The second method is almost always faster, except when the journals are written on a device which is much slower than those used to store the database. Furthermore, the new-copy journal may contain much redundant information which, as described in the last chapter, can be eliminated at intervals to reduce its length. The transaction journal cannot be reorganized in this way.

Regardless of efficiency, there are certain types of fault which new-copy reconstruction cannot handle. It can only reproduce the database as it was the instant before the failure. This is exactly what is needed if one is reasonably certain that there were no errors prior to the failure, as when the system is stopped by a major hardware breakdown. It is not good enough if, for example, a persistent program fault has been updating the files incorrectly all day. These errors will be recorded on the journals as well, so that new-copy reconstruction will reproduce them faithfully. To get rid of the errors, the transactions should be reprocessed by a corrected version of the program. When all other methods of recovery fail, reloading the database and reprocessing transactions, however long it takes, is generally still possible.

Recovery time calculations

Let us return to the example system of the last section to calculate the time required to reload and reconstruct the database in a typical situation. We will suppose that the files are dumped at the end of every day, and that on this occasion the system has failed after five hours running. The faults have been repaired, the whole database is to be reloaded and the new-copy journal is to be used to bring it up to date. Here are some more details on the disk units:

    No of cylinders: 400
    Tracks per cyl: 20
    Full track capacity: 12,600 char
    Single-cyl seek time: 10 ms

The database dumps will be organized in the most efficient way possible, each record on the tape corresponding to a full track on the disk. The maximum time to read a record from the tape is:

    $(12,600/1,200) + 10 = 20.5$ ms

The disks are reloaded as follows:

1   on the first revolution of the disk, record n (a full track) is written
2   on the second revolution, record $n - 1$ is read back and checked to make sure it was written correctly
3   On the third revolution, record $n+1$ is written, and so on.
4   at the end of a cylinder, there is an additional delay after checking the last record while the arm seeks to the next cylinder. Since the seek time of 10 ms is less than the rotation time of 16 ms, the delay is 16 ms.

The minimum time to write a full track is 32 ms and fully overlaps the tape read. The total time to reload a complete pack, therefore, is:

    $(400 \times (20 \times 32 + 16))/1000 = 262$ seconds.

Supposing that the channel capacity is insufficient to allow more than one disk to be loaded at one time, the total time to reload the database is 786 seconds, approximately 13 minutes. We will allow one minute at the beginning to mount the first dump tape, increasing the reload time to 14 minutes.

The first volume of the new-copy journal is mounted, taking another minute approximately. In the database reconstruction phase, the length of journal written in five hours normal processing must be read. This consists of:

>   450,000 type A records (800 char each)
>   200,000 type B records (300 char each)

There are 650,000 records totalling 420 million characters. The time required to write them back to the disk – assuming the records to be evenly distributed over the three units – is:

> $(1/3)[(420,000,000/800,000) + (650,000 \times (25 + 8))/1000]$
> $= 7,325$ seconds.

The maximum time required to read the journal tapes is:

> $(420,000,000/1,200,000) + ((650,000 \times 10)/1,000) = 6,850$ seconds

Again, it is the disks which are the limiting factor. If the tape reading is fully overlapped, the reconstruction phase takes 123 minutes, and the whole recovery operation takes 137 minutes, well over two hours.

This illustrates very well the point that the simple recovery scheme, reloading the whole database, may be extremely lengthy for 'a large system, and that we have to look for more sophisticated methods if rapid recovery is necessary. In this example, most of the recovery time is taken up with reprocessing the journals rather than with reloading the database, and reflects the very high transaction throughput rather than database size.

In the context of the simple recovery scheme, the only way to reduce the risk of massive file reconstructions is to dump the files more frequently, and so reduce the maximum length of journal which has to be processed. If one were to dump the files every fourteen minutes, one would clearly have no time left to do anything else, so there must be an optimum dumping frequency. In general, it depends on the performance of the hardware, the size of the database, the transaction throughput and the expected frequency of failures. This subject is explored further in chapter 7.

Exercise

a) If the system described in the example normally operates 12 hours a day, what is the average time to reload and reconstruct the database? (The database is dumped at the end of each day.)

b) A failure requiring database reconstruction occurs, on average, every 25 working days. What percentage of the time is occupied either in database recovery or routine database dumping?

c) Repeat the calculations in (a) and (b) above, assuming a dumping frequency of:

>   i   twice a day

    ii   every second day

    iii   every fifth day

6.4 Handling journal tapes

For economic reasons, journals are usually written onto magnetic tape. Without careful planning a good deal of time can be wasted in otherwise routine restarts in mounting, scanning and rewinding reels of tape. This overhead is not so noticeable in major recovery operations which take a long time in any case, but it can be a considerable nuisance in a minor restart which ought only to take two or three minutes.

In the calculations for an old-copy journal restart, we assumed that the journal tape was positioned at end-of-file after the failure. Unfortunately, this is not always the case. For a variety of reasons, the tape may be released and rewound automatically, and it must be repositioned before the restart proper can begin. Most operating systems, tidying up after aborting a user program, will close the files it had open at the time of the failure, which in the case of a tape file includes rewinding it. For this reason, the journal management routines, usually part of the data-manager should not allow themselves to be aborted if they can avoid it. They should trap as many program failures as possible so that at least they retain control of the tapes. Certain operating systems provide the facility to close a tape file without rewinding it, which the journal routines should do before closing themselves down. Nevertheless, some kinds of failure wrest control of the tape drives away from the programs without the option. Rewinding a full reel of tape and scanning to the end of it again may take three of four minutes for a high-speed drive, up to ten or fifteen minutes for a slow one.

A common rule is that, unlike disk files, tape files cannot be shared by more than one program. Often, the only way for one program to pass the file on to the next is to close it and to allow it to rewind; the second program has to start again at the beginning of the tape. The journal tapes are normally under the control of the data-manager. If a special restart program is used to manage them during recovery, the wasteful procedure of rewinding and reading from beginning to end of the file is repeated twice: once when the data-manager releases the tapes to the control of the restart program, and again at the end of the restart, when it resumes control in preparation for normal processing. This is not only wasteful of time, it duplicates programming effort, as the two programs must contain similar logic for managing the tapes. The most efficient solution is to embed the restart routines in the data-manager itself.

The delays incurred are directly proportional to the length of tape which has to be rewound and scanned. Thus, they will be negligible just after the change to a new reel of journal tape, and worst just before the end of a full reel. If the system has to be closed down, or if some kind of failure is anticipated, it can be useful to force the change to a new reel before the old one is full. This can be done by an instruction from the console operator, directly to the data-manager or via the executive program. Besides shortening the expected restart, the facility to change journal reels at will may have other uses. One might wish to force a change just *after* a restart, so that the journal up to the time of the failure is immediately available for more detailed examination and analysis.

There remains another situation which may cause unwanted tape scanning. During a restart with the old-copy journal, the recovery program may read backwards to the beginning of a reel before reaching the first checkpoint. Then the previous volume must be mounted. Before the backwards search can continue the tape has to be read through its full length to the end of the volume. The solution to this has already been suggested; the first thing to be written on each new reel should be a checkpoint.

Locating end-of-file

When the system is shut down in an orderly way, the data-manager has the opportunity to close each journal file so that the end of the file is properly marked. Thus, there is no difficulty in finding it again while reading the journals in a restart. However, many failures happen suddenly and without giving any opportunity to close the files properly, and it may not then be so easy to identify the end-of-file.

Journal writing may be interrupted half way through a record, in which case the block-check characters at the end would be missing and the recovery program would detect a parity error on attempting to read the incomplete record. A parity error is thus a possible indication of end-of-file, but not a certain one; incorrectly written records in the middle of the journal may cause the same condition. The recovery program is obliged to read further before it can decide which is the case. If the error marked the point where the system failed and where journal writing was interrupted, the recovery program will then read on to whatever was previously on the tape.

The journal tapes are usually recycled, so that today's journals may be written on tapes which were used a week or so ago and which are no longer required. There is a strong possibility, then, that the recovery program may find itself reading old journal information if it attempts to read past a parity error at the end of the current journal. It is clearly very important to be able to recognize that this information is invalid and indicates that the end-of-file has been reached. An identifying code of some kind should be associated with every record on the tape, which distinguishes current from old data. If, moreover, one adopts a scheme in which the redundant journal information is overwritten in a restart, the identifying code must be changed every time there is a restart. Otherwise, the recovery program may process records which were valid in a previous restart, have been superseded, but not yet overwritten by the current journal.

In summary, the end of the journal can be recognized by any of these events:

- a correct end-of-file condition
- a record parity error
- a change in the unique identifier associated with the current journal.

Two further methods have been suggested by Gunton (2):

- an independent count of records written should be kept, perhaps in a small disk file
- everytime a record is written to the journal, it should contain a marker indicating it to be the last one. When the next record is written, the marker in the last one is erased.

Either of these would seem likely to slow down journal writing considerably, but they might occasionally prove useful.

The journals are vital for the accurate reconstruction of the database after a failure but, like any other file, they may contain errors. What could one do if, for example, the recovery program met with a genuine parity error in the middle of a journal while attempting to restart? The possibility exists that complete records or series of records are lost as a result of hardware faults. One can check for this by including a record or cumulative character count in each record written, but what can be done if records are actually found to be missing?

Some degree of safety is provided by keeping all three logical journals separately, so that if one method of recovery fails, another can be tried. Thus, if the old-copy journal proves to be unreadable, one can attempt to reload the database and reconstruct it with the new-copy journal. Safer still, one may keep each journal in duplicate. Gaps or errors in one journal can be rectified from its copy. The overheads which journal writing imposes on normal processing are doubled, and the complexity of the recovery routines is increased considerably, since the journals have to be read in parallel and kept in step in a variety of possible error conditions.

6.5   Interface with terminal operators

The situation of a remote terminal operator during a system failure and subsequent recovery can be very confusing. The operator may not at first realize that the system has failed, and even when it becomes obvious that it is not responding correctly, he has no idea how serious the failure is or how long it will take to repair. This is a very dangerous time, when the uncertainty of the operator and the failure of some of the normal input controls of the system may introduce further errors.

It is evidently important to keep the operators as well informed as possible, and if the system closes down in an orderly way it should broadcast a message to all terminals telling them roughly how long it expects to be off the air. Whether the computer tells them about the failure or they find out for themselves, the operators should be fully trained and provided with detailed instructions on what to do until normal service is restored. There should be a clearly defined set of fallback procedures, or more than one set, depending on the severity of the failure.

The main risk of errors comes from the loss of transactions or processing the same transactions twice. Without strict controls and careful design of the interface between computer and terminal, it is easy to lose track of a transaction during a failure. At any given time, a number of messages are in process of transmission, or in the middle of application processing, or waiting in queues in main store or on disk. Some of these may be destroyed by the failure, and the terminal operator cannot be expected to know which have been applied to the files and which have not. It is up to the computer system to tell him what to do during and after recovery.

We need, therefore, to be able to identify transactions uniquely so that both the computer system and the terminal operators can tell which is which. The simplest way to do this is to assign to each a sequence number. This is used either on its own or in association with the address of the originating terminal. The latter scheme allows one also to check for missing transactions in the course of normal operation. If the computer receives a transaction numbered 105 from terminal A7 when the last one was number 103, it will immediately suspect that it has lost 104 somehow, and it can ask the operator to key it in again. If the numbers are assigned sequentially regardless of origin, the transactions arriving from a single terminal will not usually be consecutive. Thus terminal A4 may send transaction 165, followed by 166 from terminal B2, 167 from C6, 168 from B2, and 169 from A4 again. One cannot deduce anything from the fact that from terminal A4, transaction 165 was followed by 169 – the numbers must increase, but they need not be consecutive.

There are several methods by which sequence numbers can be assigned. The responsibility may be left to the terminal operators, who key in a number with the transaction, increasing it each time by one. The central system checks the number and adds the terminal address so that it has a unique code by which to refer to the message in future. This depends on the operator remembering which number to key in next.

One can avoid this if intelligent terminals are used, using the logic in the machine to calculate the number automatically. It prints or displays it for the operator's benefit, as an invitation to key in a transaction, and inserts it in the message transmitted to the central computer.

Certain types of terminal may compress several transactions into an internal buffer, to be transmitted as a single message and unpacked again on receipt. They may often be logged in their packed form as a complete message, in which case the recovery procedures need to identify messages rather than individual transactions. In this case, the sequence number of either the first or the last transaction in the message is inserted by the terminal. The difference between two successive numbers can be used to check that the correct number of transactions is found when the message is unpacked. It would be unreasonable to expect the operator to keep track of the sequence numbers here, so some logical capability in the terminal is necessary to do it.

In each case above, the sequence numbers are provided from the terminal. The central computer attaches the terminal address to form the unique identification. It has to maintain a table with an entry for each terminal, containing the next expected or the last received sequence number, which it must check and update every time a message is received. The alternative to this is to generate the number in the central system – or perhaps in some intermediate line control computer or 'front-end processor'. The number is transmitted to the terminal and printed for the operator's information.

The dialogue with the operator can be designed in various ways. The computer may send the number of the *next* transaction as an invitation to key it in, and as an acknowledgement that the previous entry was received safely. It may send the number of the *last* transaction as an acknowledgement, and implicitly to invite the entry of another one. There is no significant difference, as long as the operator knows which number belongs to which transaction. The acknowledgement generally marks the fact that the transaction has been received and logged. It may spend some time in a queue before being processed, and it is not necessary to keep the terminal waiting during that time.

When the system restarts after a failure, a number of transactions have to be reprocessed. Some of these can be recovered from the log, others may be lost completely. Let us consider a restart based on the old-copy journal. Initially, the journal is read backwards to reset the files and undo doubtful transactions. The processing state is reset from the checkpoint, which includes the table of expected sequence numbers, or the next sequence number to be allocated. The journal is read forward, picking out transactions and reprocessing them where necessary. The expected sequence numbers are updated in the normal way, as if the transactions were transmitted from terminals. Any gaps caused by errors on the journal are noted, so that the system can request the terminals to re-enter missing transactions. When the end of the journal is reached, a message is sent to each terminal telling the operator what was the number of the last good transaction received. He should start by re-entering any which have been lost, before resuming normal work.

In a well-run system, the operator may have little experience of system failure and the recovery procedures may be unfamiliar to him. Even if he is initially well-trained and provided with full instructions, he may still be uncertain what to do when a real failure arrives. His training can be supplemented and kept fresh by drills in which failure is simulated by a program in the central computer system. This may come as a regular event or as a surprise, so that the operators do not even know that it is a simulation. The drill program can monitor the reactions of each terminal operator and produce a report for a supervisor, so that deficiences in training can be corrected.

References

(1) C T Davies, *A recovery/integrity architecture for a data system*, IBM Systems Development Division, Technical report no TRO2.528, May 1972.
(2) A Gunton, *Recovery procedures for direct access commercial systems*, Computer Journal, vol 13, no 2, May 1970.

Chapter 7

Additional techniques

7.1 Single transaction recovery

In the previous chapter, the standard method of restart using the old-copy journal was described. In its simplest form, it is somewhat inefficient in that all transactions since the last checkpoint are reversed and reprocessed. Most of these will be perfectly valid; quite often, one only needs to undo those transactions which were incomplete at the time of the failure and which leave the database in an inconsistent, half-updated condition. We saw an outline in 6.2 of one way in which we could avoid reprocessing completed transactions, but as it involved scanning back to the checkpoint to find out which were complete and which were not, it did not promise much improvement in restart time.

We would like to find a more selective method, allowing the recovery of individual transactions rather than the whole batch of work since the last checkpoint. In particular, it should:

- avoid lengthy journal scans and unnecessary reprocessing after a general system failure
- allow individual programs to be restarted, without interrupting the work of programs other than the one which failed
- if a program finds that it cannot deal with a transaction, allow it to discard that transaction alone and to continue processing.

Two alternative methods may be used to recover individual transactions. First, one may delay updating until it is quite certain that the transaction has been completed successfully. Database records are retrieved and logged in the usual way, but the updates are held in a temporary working space until the updating program tells the data-manager that the transaction has finished. Only then is the database altered and the new information written to the new-copy journal. In the second method, the database is updated immediately, but the old-copy information is saved until the end of the transaction, so that it can be reversed if it cannot be completed or is interrupted for some reason. For the time being, we can assume that the working space for the recovery information or half-complete transaction is in main storage. It makes little difference to the logic of recovery where it is stored, provided that it is not destroyed in the failure.

All alterations to the database must be defined as a series of transactions. This is already the case for updates to the applications data received from the terminal network; it may be necessary to invent some special types of transaction to enforce the same discipline on changes originating in the supervisory software, such as changes to control files. In addition to requests to perform specific database operations, three control requests may be made to the data-manager from the up-date programs. They are START a transaction, FINISH a transaction, and ABORT one which has already been started but not yet finished. Each must be accompanied by the identity of the transaction to which it refers, as must the requests for database operations.

The START request warns the data-manager to expect database requests against the new transaction identity, and to allocate a working space for it. The request may be refused if, for example, the data-manager is suspending the system prior to writing a checkpoint, or if there is an error such as a duplicate transaction identity. Every time a database request is made subsequently, information is added to the working space. In the delayed update case, this is the new-copy record which is waiting to be applied to the file. If the update is made immediately, both the old and new copies are saved in the workspace. When the FINISH request is received, the delayed updates are written to the database and, in either method, the new copies are written to the journal to make a permanent record of the update. Then the transaction is deleted from the current list and the workspace is released to be used again (diagram 7.1).

If the updating program cannot finish the transaction, it issues an ABORT request. It might do this if, for example, it finds that it has received an order from a customer who does not exist, or that there is an error in the records which it has retrieved. The data-manager may abort a transaction itself if it cannot perform a database request associated with it. If the updating program fails this, too, causes the current transaction to be aborted.

Since in the delayed update method no changes have yet been made to the database, one need only divert the transaction to a suspense file where it is kept until it can be dealt with, delete it from the current list, and release the workspace. The only signs of it are some superfluous records on the old-copy journal. In the immediate update case, the old-copy images in the temporary workspace are used to reset the database, and the new-copy images are thrown away. Thus, no record of the updates is preserved on the new-copy journal.

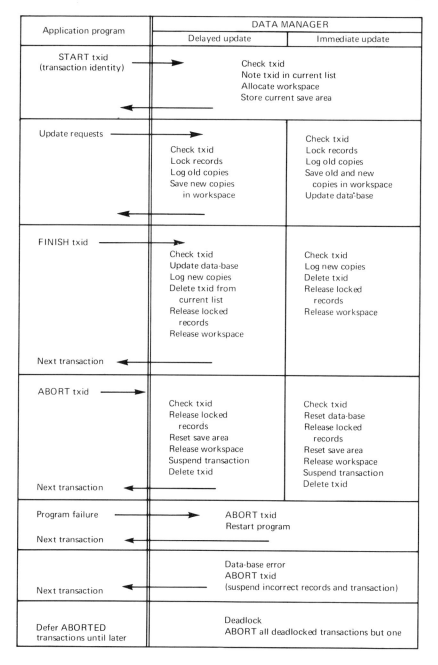

Application program	DATA MANAGER	
	Delayed update	Immediate update
START txid (transaction identity)	Check txid Note txid in current list Allocate workspace Store current save area	

Update requests	Check txid
	Lock records
	Log old copies
	Save new copies
	  in workspace
		Check txid
		Lock records
		Log old copies
		Save old and new
		  copies in workspace
		Update data-base

FINISH txid	Check txid
	Update data-base
	Log new copies
	Delete txid from
	  current list
	Release locked
	  records
	Release workspace
		Check txid
		Log new copies
		Delete txid
		Release locked
		  records
		Release workspace

Next transaction		

ABORT txid	Check txid
	Release locked
	  records
	Reset save area
	Release workspace
	Suspend transaction
	Delete txid
		Check txid
		Reset data-base
		Release locked
		  records
		Reset save area
		Release workspace
		Suspend transaction
		Delete txid

Next transaction		
Program failure Next transaction	ABORT txid Restart program	
Next transaction	Data-base error ABORT txid (suspend incorrect records and transaction)	
Defer ABORTED transactions until later	Deadlock ABORT all deadlocked transactions but one	

7.1   Program discipline

In either scheme, all records updated in the course of a transaction must be locked and reserved for the exclusive use of the program processing it. Otherwise, there is a danger that two programs might retrieve the same record from the database and update it independently. When they come to complete their respective transactions, the program which finished last would overwrite the changes made by the other program. Records must be locked for the duration of the whole transaction, which may involve the alteration of several other records. Each is locked for longer, on average, than in the simple system where they are locked, updated and released individually. The chance that a program will have to wait for a locked record, and the average time spent so waiting, will be increased proportionately. This should only become a serious problem if a transaction involves some dialogue with the terminal operator; then records may be locked out for minutes at a time, rather than for fractions of a second.

Thus, the discipline required by single transaction recovery increases the risk of deadlocks. It also provides a simple mechanism to resolve them, however. When a deadlock is detected, the data-manager can pre-empt the records required for the completion of one of the transactions by aborting the others. A program whose transaction is aborted is told the reason (through a return code of some kind), and it will defer the transaction and try to process it again later. Several methods may be used to decide which transactions are to be aborted and which is to be allowed to complete. The decision may be made on allocated priorities, or the number of records each program has already secured, or the length of time each has been in progress.

ABORTs can be requested by application programs, or enforced by the data-manager which will notify the application program and state the reason for it so that the program can take suitable action. In general, it will defer the transaction until later or ignore it and get on with the next one. If the program actually fails, the data data-manager can still abort its current transaction without difficulty but it must also restart the program. It must, moreover, do it without upsetting other programs, which means that the failed program must be restarted from the beginning of its current transaction. Any work which it undertook in previous transactions may since have been used by other programs, and cannot be reversed without restarting the whole system.

Enough information must be preserved by each application program to enable it to be restarted after any transaction. This includes, for example, running totals and statistics which must be accumulated and carried forward from one transaction to the next. One might keep it in control files maintained as part of the database, at the expense of some extra I/O overhead. An alternative method suggested here is that all such information is kept in a special data structure, which we will call the *application* save area, shared by the program and the data-manager, but owned by the latter. Thus, it is preserved even when the application program fails. Only temporary working information relevant to the current transaction is stored by the program itself.

If an application program is allowed to update its save area in the course of a transaction, it will not usually be valid if the transaction is aborted. Nor is it possible to ensure the consistency of the save area by requiring the program to update it at the end of the transaction; the program may still be interrupted while it is in process of altering the save area, which will then be invalid. The probability of this is small but finite, and therefore cannot be ignored. The problem can be solved easily by taking a copy of the save area at the start of the transaction, and putting it in the workspace along with the old-copy database records. If the transaction has to be aborted, this can be used to reset the save area to its original state.

One save area is assigned to each program currently processing. When a new program is scheduled, a fresh area of the appropriate format is assigned, or an area preserved from a previous execution of the program is read back in from a control file. When a program finishes 'execution, the corresponding save area is written away for future use, or is perhaps accumulated into a summary file. Every time a checkpoint is taken, the save areas for all programs currently in execution are included.

Thus, we have met the second and third objectives we set for a single transaction recovery scheme. How can we use it to recover from a general system failure, such as might be caused by a processor fault or an interruption in the power supply? First of all we should note that the scheme in no way prevents the conventional methods of recovery depending on the record and transaction journals, as described in chapter 6. If ever single transaction recovery fails – as it might if, for example, information in a save area or a workspace were found to be in error – one can revert to a full old-copy journal restart or, if necessary, to database reconstruction.

Let us first suppose that the contents of main storage are not destroyed by the failure. The workspaces will show a number of transactions in various stages of progress. Those which are not yet finished are aborted. Others will be complete, but the updates may not yet have been written to the database or to the new-copy journal. The recovery routine forces the completion of these transactions by copying the new-copy records in the workspaces to the database and the journal. In fact, the system can be restarted entirely from the workspaces and the save areas, without reference to the checkpoint or journal files except, where necessary, to reposition them ready for continued processing.

The situation is somewhat different if the contents of main storage are lost. As we have already noted, the logic of recovery is largely independent of the medium on which the workspaces are kept; nothing that has been described so far is changed if they are kept on a high-speed disk or drum, and we can still retrieve them even after a failure which destroys main storage. The workspaces can be used as before to reset some incomplete transactions and to force the completion of the others. All current save areas must be kept on disk as well. These are updated by the data-manager from the main storage versions when the FINISH request is received for each transaction.

This, unfortunately, is not all that one needs to restart the system. One can restore the database to a consistent state and reset the application programs, but one still has to determine which transactions are next to be processed and to recover any which may have been lost in main storage queues. This can usually only be done by returning to a checkpoint and scanning forward along the transaction journal, noting those received from each terminal and, from the completion markers, those which have been processed. To get any advantage from this the checkpoint file, the transaction journal and the old-copy journal must be maintained as separate files, otherwise one must in any case scan backwards down the journal to find the checkpoint.

There are some occasions on which the system can be restarted very quickly after a general failure using the single transaction recovery technique. Usually, however, it does not give very much help, and it must be measured against the continuous I/O overhead incurred by keeping the workspaces and save areas on disk or drum. If they are kept in main storage, the only significant overhead at run-time is the amount of space they take up. One must then accept that most general system failures will require a full-scale restart, using at least the checkpoint and old-copy journal.

7.2   Efficient file reconstruction

A common cause of system failures, in some systems the most common, is faulty disk storage. As a result, it often happens that part of the database is damaged or cannot be read, and has to be reconstructed. The method of recovery using the old-copy journal described in 6.2 is ineffective, since some of the lost records may not have been updated for days or weeks and no copy of them is preserved on the journal. However, the other methods at our disposal require the database to be completely reloaded from a dump and all work done since to be reprocessed. This is a drastic solution if only a small part of the database is affected as, in a large system, it may take hours. Indeed, the example worked through in 6.3 showed a time of more than two hours even to reconstruct quite a small database. We would like some method of partial reconstruction which works only on the faulty areas of the database, and leaves the unaffected parts alone.

Modified new-copy technique

A situation which will often arise is that a specific storage device fails, and either it cannot be repaired immediately or the data on it cannot be recovered. On a smaller scale, the failure may affect a track, cylinder, sector or some other subdivision of a whole storage unit. We need to reconstruct a physical area of the database rather than a logical one. It is easier to modify the new-copy journal method of recovery for this purpose than the transaction journal method. Database records can be identified as belonging in a specific storage area, but transactions may refer to records in one or more logical files, physically scattered all over the storage space. Thus, a transaction which accesses data in the damaged areas may also access data in other areas, which must be reloaded as well before the transaction can be reprocessed.

To effect a partial reconstruction we must be able to:

– identify the areas which are inaccessible or contain errors
– reload selectively from a recent dump only the affected areas
– during reconstruction with the new-copy journal, pick out and re-write records relating only to the affected areas, ignoring all others.

The first requirement is by no means trivial. Often the failure may be accompanied by a message at the console which says that a record at a certain address on a certain disk unit cannot be read, but this only specifies the record which caused the immediate failure and does not give the full extent of the errors. One may obtain some relevant information from the data-manager, which keeps, for example, a list of records which it has had to lock out because they contain errors, or one may run a diagnostic program which checks suspect areas of the database and reports any errors it finds.

The way in which areas of the database are described and addressed presents some problems. Application programs generally refer to records by some logical key, for instance, "the account record for customer #216483". The data-manager will use a form which can be used more efficiently by the direct file access methods supporting the logical organization visible to the application. Typically, this form is a relative record number within a physical file, which need not coincide with the files known to the application program. It is used to identify records on journal tapes, and in the data-manager's internal control tables. Finally, our selective recovery programs must be able to recognize hardware addresses such as "disk unit #34" or "cylinder 114 of unit 126". The recovery programs must determine whether a particular record on the journal, identified by its file and relative record number, belongs to one of the physical areas it is reconstructing. Either we must do the translation for it in advance, or it must do it for itself.

The second requirement for partial reconstruction tells us how the database dump should be organized. Since one wants to retrieve the data belonging to particular physical areas, that is the way it should be dumped. The contents of one disk pack, for example, will be dumped continuously to one or more tape volumes. One does not always have to reload the contents of a complete unit; sometimes it is only one track of a disk which is needed, and one wants to reload this on its own. Clearly, some kind of directory is required to locate a given area on a particular tape volume.

For a relatively simple system, this might be no more than a list printed by the dump program. The operators refer to it in deciding which volume of the dump to mount, and the reload program picks out the area that it wants from wherever it is stored on the tape. For a large database dumped on many volumes of tape, a machine-readable directory is preferable. It would contain not only the location of database areas on the dump tapes, but also the physical addresses at which particular ranges of records were stored. Output from the data-manager or the diagnostic program could thus be translated automatically, so that the operators need do nothing except mount the tapes requested by the reload program (diagram 7.2). If the directory also contains the position on each reel of any given database area, the time spent searching the tapes can be minimized by asking the operators to mount the tapes in order of decreasing expected search time.

The modified reconstruction procedure is quite simple (diagram 7.3). Every record on the new-copy journal is marked with the file and relative record number which specifies where it belongs in the database. As the journals are read during the reconstruction phase, records which belong in the damaged areas are re-written in the database, the rest are ignored. As in the simple method this continues until the end of the tape or until a suitable checkpoint, and recovery is completed with an old-copy journal restart. One problem remains: the reconstruction program has to select those records which correspond to particular hardware addresses, which must be translated into file and record number form. It could do this itself by referring to the dump directory. In diagram 7.2, however, the diagnostic program is shown as producing a recovery directory which is an extract of the information relevant to the damaged areas only. It contains the information that the reload program needs to retrieve the appropriate sections of the dump, as well as a specification of the areas to be recovered in the form of file and record number ranges, for the benefit of the reconstruction program.

Modified technique - advantages

We have described some simple modifications to the new-copy journal recovery method. What does this technique gain us? Only a part, possibly a small part, of the database need be reloaded, instead of all of it. This is a considerable advantage if the database is very large. However, we still

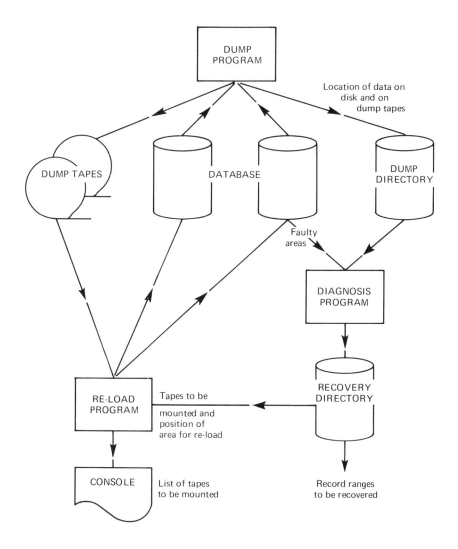

7.2   Selective database reload

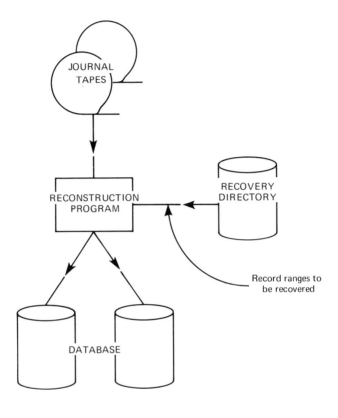

7.3   Selective reconstruction

have to process sequentially the whole of the new-copy journal from the time of the dump to the time of the failure. This could be dozens of reels of tape. If only a small area of the database is recovered, relevant records may be scattered few and far between on the journal. Although we only have to write the relevant records back to the database, we still have to read all of the irrelevant ones.

Let us consider how this affects the example of 6.3. We need to know, now, rather more facts about the database and how it is distributed. We will suppose that two packs contain type A records, of length 800 characters, and the third contains type B records of 300 characters.

Allowing for inter-record gaps on the disk, a single track will hold 14 type A or 30 type B records, approximately. There are about 180,000 records in file A and 200,000 in file B (the packs are not completely full).

Suppose, now, that the system fails after five hours running, as before. A single track of file B records is found to be at fault. Thus, only 30 records have to be recovered. Some of these may have been updated several times in the period since the dump. However, from the transaction volumes (given in section 5.5) we see that there are about 40,000 'hits' per hour on file B, or 200,000 in five hours. If the failed track was representative of the whole file, not containing any particularly heavily accessed records, there will be about 30 records belonging to the failed track on the journal tapes.

The reload phase now involves mounting a single tape only, and searching it until the relevant track is found. Assuming that the search is at the maximum tape transport speed of 200 inches per second, and that the track is about half way up the tape, it takes about 72 seconds to find it, and at most a few seconds to read it and restore it to the disk. Allowing a minute to mount the tape, as before, the reload phase takes about 2 minutes instead of 14 minutes for the whole database.

We are still obliged to read the whole new-copy journal, 650,000 records totalling 420 million characters of data. Since most of the records on the tapes are ignored, we can assume that it is possible to drive them at near their maximum speed of 200 inches per second. Thus, for the start-stop time of 10 ms we can substitute an inter-block gap time which will be about half, or 5 ms. The total time required to read the journal is:

$$(420,000,000/1,200,000) + ((650,000 \times 5)/1,000) = 3,600 \text{ seconds}$$

The journal-reading phase takes a total of 61 minutes including set-up time, and the whole reconstruction about 63 minutes. This is less than half the time required for a full database reconstruction, which was limited by the speed at which records could be written back to the disk. In this case, we are limited by the speed at which the tapes can be read. If the journal is unblocked, as we have continued to assume, a great amount of space is taken up by the gaps between records, one inch or 6000 characters for each. Five hours of new-copy journal occupies 60,000 feet of tape, twenty-five standard reels. Less than 10% of this is new-copy information; the rest is gap.

Exercise

How would the restart time be improved in the example above if the new-copy journal were written in blocks of average size 4000 characters? 8000 characters?

Audit trail tag file

The modified technique outlined above is an improvement on the basic method in which the whole database has to be reloaded, but it still needs to read the whole of the new-copy journal from beginning to end, in the order in which it was written. If it were possible to process several journal tapes in parallel, the recovery time would be greatly reduced. However, since there may be several versions of the same record in the journal, it is essential that the most recent be the last to be written back to the database, and this normally requires that the journal be read sequentially in its original order. There is a technique which can be used to circumvent this requirement. It involves the use of an extra file called the Audit Trail Tag File (ATTF).

The ATTF contains one record for every record in the new-copy journal, and is written by the data-manager in the course of normal operation as it logs updated records on the journal. In its simplest form, each record contains only two items of information:

–   the identity of the updated record (file number and relative record number)
–   the location of the record on the new-copy journal (tape reel number and record number).

The ATTF records are fixed in size and very small. They could be compressed into two binary words, or eight to twelve characters. The file is therefore much smaller than the new-copy journal of which it is an image. To return to our example system, an average of 130,000 new-copy records are written in an hour. The ATTF file for a full twelve hour day, assuming twelve characters per record, would occupy less than 19 million characters. It could thus be kept entirely on disk, perhaps in duplicate for security. To achieve a reasonable file size, however, the records would have to be grouped together in fairly large blocks. There is then the likelihood that a number of them would be lost in a failure. This does not affect the recovery procedure described below provided any incomplete blocks are written out whenever a checkpoint is taken. Then the old-copy journal restart which concludes the recovery will take care of any errors introduced by losing records at the end of the new-copy journal.

In the event of a failure, the ATTF is used to aid database reconstruction, as follows (diagram 7.4):

1   As before, the areas to be reconstructed are decided on information provided by the diagnosis program.
2   While the required areas are being reloaded, the records in the ATTF file which correspond to the areas to be reconstructed are extracted. They are sorted in order of their database file and record number and duplicates are eliminated by discarding all but the most recent (the one with the highest tape location).

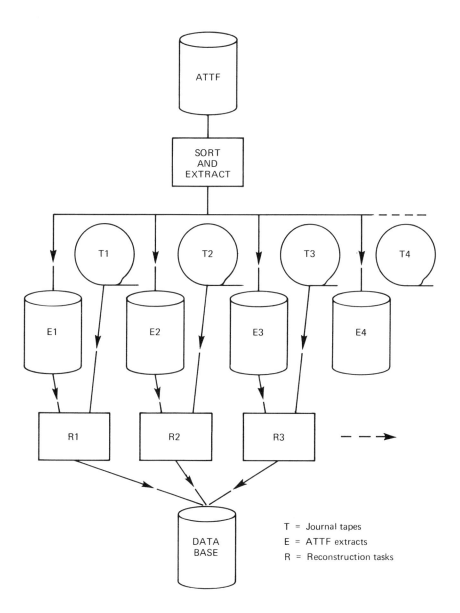

7.4   Reconstruction with ATTF

3   The extracted records are sorted back into tape location order and divided into groups by tape reel number. Only those tapes which appear in the extract file need be processed.

4   A number of tasks are initiated, each of which processes a separate reel of tape. The number of tapes which can be handled efficiently at one time depends on the computer configuration, in particular on the number of tape drives available and on the channel capacity. On a large system it may be possible to drive six or more tapes at near their maximum speed. Each task retrieves every record on its reel which corresponds to one of the extracted ATTF records, and restores it to the database.

5   When all the tapes have been processed the system begins as before with a normal old-copy journal restart.

This method is an enormous improvement over the technique described at the beginning of this section. Since redundant copies of multiply-updated records are eliminated at the ATTF sort stage, the tape does not have to be processed sequentially. The multi-programming power of the computer can be used to process a number of essentially I/O-bound tasks in parallel, reducing the reconstruction time to a fraction of the time it would otherwise take. In fact, some journal reels may not need to be processed at all. Against this must be set the overheads incurred by the ATTF, both during recovery and in normal operation. These should usually be small. If the ATTF records are grouped in large blocks, the I/O overheads in normal running should be negligible by comparison with those incurred by the new-copy journal itself. The only significant extra work required during recovery is to extract and sort the ATTF records. This proceeds in parallel with reloading sections of the database, and does not usually have any effect on the total recovery time.

Recovery time calculations

To support the claims made for the ATTF method, let us apply it to the example system to find the improvement in recovery time. On this occasion, however, we will also suppose that the new-copy journal is written in blocks of average size 8000 characters. As before, the system fails after five hours' running when a track of file B records is found to be unreadable and, also as before, the file reload phase takes a little more than two minutes.

While the reload is in progress, the ATTF file is read sequentially to extract records relating to the bad track. By this time, there are about 650,000 records in the ATTF, and we shall suppose each is 12 characters long, written in blocks of 200 records. There should thus be five 2,400 character blocks on a track. The entire file occupies 650 tracks, nearly 33 cylinders. The time required to read the file sequentially, supposing a full rotation delay between each block is:

(data transfer) + (rotational delay) + (seek)
= ((650,000 × 12)/800,000) + ((3,250 × 16)/1,000) + ((32 × 10)/1,000)
= 62 seconds

We estimated previously that about 30 records would be relevant to the track which had failed. To sort these, eliminate duplicates and sort them back into tape location order could scarcely take more than a few seconds. Thus, our assumption that the ATTF extraction and sort would be overlapped by the data base reload is shown to be justified in this particular case.

We now need to know how much tape the blocked new-copy journal occupies. There are:

420,000,000/8,000 = 52,500 blocks.

These occupy:

(420,000,000/(6,000 × 12)) + (52,500/12) = 10,200 feet.

The journal has just started on its fifth reel since the database dump. Five programs can be set off to read them all in parallel. To read from one end of a tape to the other at maximum speed takes 144 seconds. If we suppose that it takes three minutes to mount the tapes, the total time for the journal-reading phase – when the last-mounted tape has been read to the end – is about five minutes. The whole database reconstruction takes seven or eight minutes.

It should be remembered that, in all the recovery time calculations we have made so far, we have left out the time for the old-copy journal restart with which database reconstruction is usually concluded. It is of no relevance to the comparison between the various methods of new-copy journal reconstruction, but it must be added to give a true figure for the total restart time. In section 6.2, an average time of four minutes was found (on the basis of an *unblocked* old-copy journal).

In the situation we have considered here, the ATTF technique allows normal service to be restored in eleven or twelve minutes from the time of setting the recovery procedure in motion. Although the actual figure is not of any great interest, since it depends on the characteristics of an imaginary and much-simplified example system, the improvement over the basic method is quite dramatic.

7.3   Optimum dumping frequency

Let us return briefly to the simple new-copy journal method of reconstruction described in 6.3, and in particular to the question of choosing how often to dump the files. At one extreme, if one were to dump the files very rarely or not at all, then new-copy journal recovery would be very lengthy or impossible. At the other extreme, if one were to dump the files very frequently the system would spend all its time dumping files and none doing useful work. Somewhere in between we hope to find an optimum frequency in any particular case; and we want to know what characteristics of a real-time system are important in determining the optimum, and how to calculate it.

First, however, we must decide precisely what we mean by 'optimum'. It is the best result we can get from the trade-off between the time spent on recovery and the time spent on dumping. We want the computer system to spend the greatest possible proportion of its time in normal, productive working. Then the optimum dumping frequency is the one which gives, on average over a long period, a minimum value to:

   (dumping time + recovery time)/(total running time)

or, equivalently, to:

   (dumping time + recovery time)/(time spent on normal working).

Clearly, the choice of dumping frequency is restricted by the operational characteristics of the system. If we obtain a result from our calculations which tells us to dump the files every 71 hours 9 minutes, when we know that it has to be done some time at night between 11pm and 3am, then we will have to bend the result to fit the actual situation. Nevertheless, the same basic principles apply to the decision as if we were free to choose the theoretical ideal.

We will start by picking out the aspects of the system which seem to be important in determining the value of the optimum. First, the average time spent on dumping depends on the size of the database and on the performance of the available hardware and software. The average time spent on recovery depends on the frequency with which failures occur and the average time it takes to recover from a single failure, and this in its turn is composed of a fixed part – the time required to set up the recovery operation and to reload the files – and a variable part which is roughly proportional to the amount of work which has to be reprocessed. This is where the main dependence between dumping frequency and recovery time comes in. The greater the interval between dumps, the greater is the average amount of work which has to be reprocessed; in fact, we can suppose that the average failure happens half-way between dumps.

In all that follows,

   D = time to dump the database (assumed to be the same as the reload
         time),
   W = normal working time between successive dumps,
   R = average time spent on recovery between successive dumps,
   S = set-up time for a recovery operation
   A = average time to recover from one failure,
   F = mean working time between failures.

We are only considering failures which require reconstruction with the new-copy journal. Minor failures are ignored, as recovery from them is independent of dumping frequency. Before embarking on some calculations for the general case, let us see how these variables behave in the example worked in section 6.3. D was calculated to be 14 minutes, and the recovery time for a failure ocurring after 5 hours of normal running was made up as follows:

14 minutes to reload the files
1 minute to set up the journals
122 minutes to process the journals

To find the *average* recovery time, A, we simply note that the time taken to reprocess the journals is proportional to the working time since the dump. Thus, if W is 12 hours, the average recovery time is calculated as if the system failed after six hours running, and is

14 minutes reload time,
1 minute set up time,
146 minutes reprocessing time $((6 \times 122)/5)$
161 minutes in total.

Let us suppose now that a failure requiring this kind of reconstruction occurs every 25 working days, on average. Then F = 300 hours. The average time per day spent on recovery is thus:

$(161 \times 12)/300 = 6.4$ minutes

The ratio of dumping and recovery time to normal working time is:

$(14 + 6.4)/(12 \times 60) = 0.0283$

We can repeat these calculations for any chosen dumping frequency, and table 7.1 shows the results tabulated for frequencies of 6, 12, 18, 24, 36, 48 and 60 hours, represented also in graph form in diagram 7.5. The minimum appears to be near W = 18 hours, but dumping daily (W = 12 hr) or every second day (W = 24 hr) give results quite close to the minimum.

W		A	R	D + R	$\dfrac{D + R}{W}$
working					
days	hours	minutes	minutes	minutes	
0.5	6	88	1.8	15.8	0.044
1.0	12	161	6.4	20.4	0.028
1.5	18	235	13.1	27.1	0.025
2.0	24	308	24.6	38.6	0.027
3.0	36	454	54.5	68.5	0.032
4.0	48	600	96	110	0.038
5.0	60	747	149	163	0.045

Table 7.1   Effect of varying dump frequency

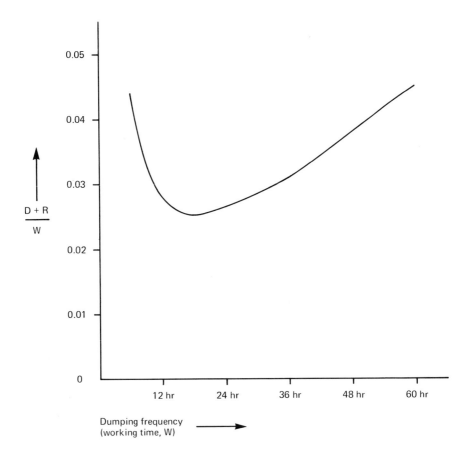

7.5   Variation of dumping and recovery time with dumping frequency

The basis of all these calculations was the result that we obtained in
chapter 6, namely, that it takes on average 122 minutes to reprocess 5
hours of work. This result in itself was the end product of some fairly
detailed calculations, but having once obtained it the rest followed by
simple proportionality. This suggests a very simple way of expressing the
recovery time r in the general case, as a function of the working time w
since the last file dump:

$r = D + S + pw$

D and S are the file reload and set up times as before, and p is a constant which, to a good approximation, is fixed for any particular real-time system, determined by the recovery technique used, the type and volume of transactions, and the hardware characteristics. It is, in fact:

(normal average transaction throughput)÷(transaction reprocessing rate during recovery).

It can be regarded as a measure of how fast the system can catch up with lost time during recovery. We will call it the *recovery speed factor*. In the example system, it is $(122/300) = 0.41$.

Now let us consider the general case. This will involve some relatively simple mathematics which reluctant readers may skip if they wish. We start by expressing the average recovery time for a single failure as an instance of the general recovery time given in the equation above:

$A = D + S + 0.5pW$

since the average value of w is 0.5W.

We want to find a minimum value for $(D + R)/W = x$.

Now R is the average time spent on recovery in one dump cycle, so $R = (A \times W)/F$. Thus:

$x = (1/W)(D + (D + S + 0.5pW)(W/F))$
$\quad = (D/W) + (1/F)(D + S + 0.5pW)$

x is a function of W, since D, S, F and p are fixed. In order to find its minimum, we differentiate x with respect to W and find a zero value.

$dx/dW = -(D/W^2) + (p/2F)$

When x is at a minimum, $(D/W^2) = (p/2F)$ or $W = \sqrt{(2DF/p)}$. Mathematically minded readers can prove for themselves that this is a minimum and not a maximum.

Let us consider the significance of this equation. It recommends a dumping frequency which will minimize the time wasted on recovery and dumping, provided that we know D, F and p. D is fairly easy to calculate from the hardware speed and the database size, or it can be measured by a simple experiment; p can also be calculated, though it requires rather detailed consideration of the characteristics and distribution of the transaction types processed by the system, and of the mechanism of recovery. F, however, is not easy to obtain theoretically. It can be deduced from observing the system over a long period and collecting statistics on the type and frequency of failures which actually occur.

In actual cases, the ideal value so obtained may often be overridden by more pressing operational considerations. It is, however, applicable in more complex circumstances where it may prove useful. In the next section we discuss systems in which parts of the database are dumped with different frequencies, and we can use the formula to derive optimum frequencies for each section. It can be extended to any recovery technique in which recovery time is proportional to the time since the last dump.

In all our calculations, we considered only failures which require the database to be reloaded and the new-copy or transaction journals to be reprocessed. Minor failures, however, are usually dealt with using the old-copy journals. At first sight, this may appear to render the calculations irrelevant, but this is not so; they need only be adjusted slightly. The definition of W, 'working time between successive dumps', should be adjusted by a factor which allows for the amount of time consumed by minor restarts. Thus, in the example system the uncorrected formula gives:

$$W = \sqrt{((2 \times 14 \times 25 \times 12)/(60 \times 0.41))} = 18.5 \text{ hours}$$

If we suppose that an average of one hour on top of each 12 hour working day is occupied by minor restarts, we should recalculate this as follows, considering W as 'working time plus minor restart time'

$$W = \sqrt{((2 \times 14 \times 25 \times 13)/(60 \times 0.41))} = 19.2 \text{ hours}$$

which represents $(19.2 \times 12)/13 = 17.75$ hours of actual working time. Since operational convenience would, in any case, probably require 12 or 24 hours rather than 18, this scarcely makes an important difference.

What is more important is to observe that the old-copy journal technique can itself be subjected to a very similar analysis, to determine the optimum frequency for checkpoints. This formula results:

$$Y = \sqrt{(2CG/q)} \text{ where}$$

Y is the optimum checkpoint frequency;
C is the working time lost by taking a checkpoint;
G is the mean working time between minor failures;
q is the recovery speed factor for OCJ restarts.

Note that p and q are not equal. In our consideration of the performance of the OCJ restart, we concluded that it took four minutes to recover after three minutes of working time, in the example system. q is therefore roughly 1.33. Taking representative values for C and G of 3 seconds and 6 hours respectively:

$$Y = \sqrt{((2 \times 3 \times 6 \times 60)/(60 \times 1.33))} = 5.2 \text{ minutes.}$$

Exercise

The recovery speed factors used above were calculated on the basis of unblocked old and new copy journals. Recalculate the RSF for both types of restart, assuming this time that the journals are written in 8000 character blocks. Using the same values for C, D, F, G as before, calculate the new optimum dump and checkpoint frequency.

7.4 Non-contemporary file dumps

As we observed earlier, the simplest method of dumping the database, both from the operational and the system design points of view, is to dump it all at once. However, we have already seen that for more efficient recovery, we may want to divide the dump into sections which can be reloaded and reconstructed independently. This can be achieved with a single, contemporary dump suitably organized, but it is only a

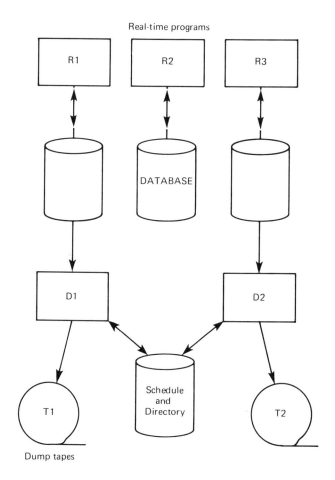

7.6   Continuous dumping

small extra step to allow the dump sections to be written at different times and at various frequencies.

The dumping and recovery procedures may then become extremely complicated, and one would only adopt a dumping system of this kind for a very good reason. Some of the circumstances under which a single dump cannot be used have previously been mentioned: the database is so large that it would take far too long to dump it all at once; there is no time for a full dump because the system has to be on the air continuously; there are wide variations in the level of activity in various parts of the database, so not all sections need to be dumped with the same frequency.

In the scheme to be described here, we dispense with the notion that the system must be stopped when the files are dumped and then started afresh. Instead, dumping is carried out by processes which run concurrently with the real-time system, copying segments of the database according to a master schedule. The boundaries of database sections, the locations of current and previous generations of dump elements and the time at which they were taken are all held in a directory which is shared by the dumping and recovery procedures (diagram 7.6). The schedule may be worked out in advance, or it may be modified dynamically according to activity on the database.

How, then, does one construct the schedule – that is to say, how does one decide how to divide up the database, and how frequently to dump each section? It is difficult to put forward any formal method for partitioning the database. For reasons of efficiency, the dump sections are likely to be physically contiguous ranges of records corresponding to a convenient subdivision of a storage unit. If the sections are too small, the dump management overheads will be heavy, while if they are too large the advantages of localized recovery may be lost. Beyond that, little positive guidance can be given. However, having once decided on the partition, one can choose the optimum dumping frequency by a formula similar to the one shown in the last section. The derivation is not given here, but it proceeds along the same lines as before. The optimum frequency W is given by:

$W = \sqrt{(2/pkf)}$ where

p = recovery speed factor, as before

k = dump/reload speed, in characters per second

f = error incidence rate, in errors per character per second

To illustrate the meaning of the last, suppose that there is an average of one error on a 100 million byte disk pack every 300 hours. Then:

$f = 1/(10^8 \times 300 \times 3600) \simeq 9.3 \times 10^{-15}$

Then if p, for an efficient reconstruction method, were 0.05, and k were 300,000 characters/second, the recommended W would be:

$\sqrt{((2 \times 1.08 \times 10^{14})/(0.05 \times 3 \times 10^5))} = 1.2 \times 10^5$ seconds

$(\simeq 33$ hours)

Two things are worthy of note about this formula. The first is that, if we regard the whole database as a single dump section of size K characters, the above formula is exactly equivalent to the one of the previous section, for:

$$D = (K/k) \text{ and } F = (1/Kf)$$
$$\text{so } \sqrt{(2DF/p)} = \sqrt{(2/pkf)}$$

The other interesting characteristic is that the optimum dumping frequency is independent of section size. p and k are constants for the system, and the formula depends only on f, the local error incidence rate. This is why different dumping frequencies are appropriate for different sections of the database. Areas which are accessed very infrequently will have a much lower error incidence rate than areas which are heavily accessed; the former should be dumped less frequently than the latter.

Ideally, one would like to be able to express all the relevant characteristics of the database, together with constraints such as the maximum permitted dumping load on the channels, and feed them into a utility program. This would produce a schedule and directory specifying the database partition, the optimum dump frequencies and the organization of the dump to minimise expected recovery time. Some of the rules it used would be of the kind just shown, others would be rules of thumb. One would need to feed in rather detailed information about the layout of the database, the performance and reliability of the devices on which it is stored and the pattern of database access.

Much of this information, unfortunately, is not available at the systems design stage, so the first attempt is bound to be based on a certain amount of guesswork. However, during testing and live running, statistics will be collected for tuning the dump and recovery system. The dump directory can be used to accumulate information on the actual pattern of access and error incidence, by dump section, so that the schedule can be adjusted dynamically.

We now need to consider how we can dump a section of the database while the real-time system is still running and updating it at the same time. In particular, need we lock out a section of the database while it is being dumped? This might impose delays of several minutes on some transactions, and is to be avoided if possible. In fact, it proves not to be necessary, provided that each dump section can be associated with the extent of the new-copy journal which was written while the dump was taken. If updates are allowed on the section being dumped, it may happen that some of the records which have already been copied will be updated before the dump is complete, so that it does not represent a consistent picture of the database section at any particular time. However, this does not matter, as the inconsistency is resolved when the journal tapes are processed. If we ensure that all journal records following the *start* of the file dump are rewritten, then by the time that the end of the section dump is reached, and at all times thereafter, that section of the database will be consistent again.

Each section is associated in the dump directory with the time at which the dump started and the time at which it ended. To be more exact, each is associated with two new-copy journal volume and record numbers – the last record written before the dump commenced, and the first one after it ended. Before recovery can begin, we need to know which parts of the database have to be reloaded. The information provided by the data-manager and the diagnostic program is translated, using the dump directory, into a set of sections to be reloaded. The most recent version of each section is selected whose dump terminated before the checkpoint chosen for the restart. A number of tasks can be despatched to restore several sections in parallel.

When all necessary areas of the database have been reloaded, the new-copy journal is processed as in the basic NCJ recovery, but starting with the volume current at the start of the *earliest* dump section reloaded. Each record on the journal is examined to see which section it belongs to, and is only written back to the database if the journal record was written after the start of the corresponding dump. This is determined simply by comparing its volume and record number with that in the directory. Finally, recovery is completed with an old-copy journal restart.

The audit trail tag file can be used to good effect in this form of recovery, just as in the simpler form of reconstruction described in 7.2. It works in just the same way, eliminating new copy redundancies and allowing several reels of journal to be processed in parallel. No changes need to be made to the ATTF records. The only change in the procedure is to use the dump directory to eliminate all records in the reloaded areas which were written prior to the corresponding section dump. This is done by simple comparison of the volume/record number in the ATTF with the directory entries.

Chapter 8

Conclusion -
designing the system

So far, this book has been devoted to presenting a set of concepts for integrity and recovery, and describing a number of alternative strategies and techniques. To turn this into a complete methodology for recovery system design, we would need to produce a comprehensive checklist of the decisions one must make in relation to integrity and recovery, who makes them, when and how. We do not attempt anything so ambitious in this final chapter and, in fact, it would be misleading to do so. We have tried to avoid the suggestion that there is anything which can be identified as a distinct "recovery subsystem", a component of the overall computer system which can be cleanly detached from the rest. On the countrary, the decisions one has to make are bound up with the whole process of system design and development, and here we only try to suggest how integrity and recovery fit into the overall picture.

In diagram 8.1 we show what is perhaps the simplest model possible for the development of a system. It is adapted from Waters' *Introduction to Computer Systems Design* (NCC Publications, 1974). The first phase – analysis and definition – is to find out what the system is for and what it has to do, and the output is a set of documents setting out the objectives of the system and its information processing requirements in considerable detail. One may sometimes go through an initial feasibility study stage in which one carries out the analysis at a fairly general level, before deciding to proceed to a more detailed study. From the specification produced by the analysts, one can produce a system design. This is not only a computer system design; the object is to produce a complete information system, which must include the human system which surrounds the computer and the interfaces between them.

123

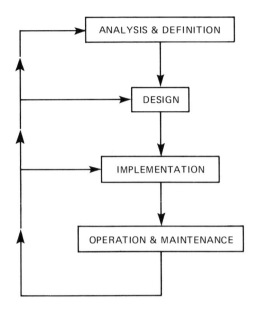

8.1   The system development process

Even supposing that the system is implemented exactly according to its
design specification, one still faces the prospect that it may not do exactly
what is required of it or that the user may change his mind about what he
wants – either because his needs have changed, or because he did not
really know what he wanted in the first place. The development process is
iterative, and we can go back from any stage to a previous one. If a
particular design proves too complicated to implement or too difficult to
operate, we go back and design something simpler. If it does not reach its
performance objectives, we go back and tune it. If we cannot predict the
behaviour of some part of the system without knowing more about the
input data, we go and get the information we need.

The iterative nature of the development process makes the divisions
between the four stages rather fluid. At times, and even with the most
disciplined methods of system development and project control, one may
feel unsure whether one is implementing a particular part of the system,
designing it, or still deciding what it is supposed to do. Indeed, the best
systems designers sometimes do all three at once. However, the four
stages are quite useful as a broad picture, and the checklist (table 8.1 at
the end of the chapter) identifies 'things to do' at each stage of the

development of the integrity and recovery parts of the system. Diagram 8.2 is an expansion of the first, very simple picture, and shows how the activities and decisions in the checklist fit into the overall pattern of system development. It is most important to remember that the *decisions one makes in designing the integrity and recovery procedures are not only technical decisions* depending on the file organisations or processing methods chosen. *They are dependent on the requirements of the users of the system*, as we emphasized in chapter 2.

The behaviour of any realistic computer system is very complicated, and there is a multitude of design decisions and alternatives, many of which interact with one another. In particular, the alternatives we select for integrity and recovery can have a considerable effect on the cost and performance of the whole system. Fortunately, we do not usually have to try a particular solution on a full-scale system to find out how it will perform, and we have a number of ways of modelling the behaviour of different proposals. In fact, we have discussed a number of recovery techniques in some detail in the preceding chapters, and have tried to predict how they behave in practice. Thus, we can say that we have made simple models of parts of the recovery system. This was only possible by making assumptions which are at best approximately true, in order to simplify recovery to the point where it is accessible to elementary algebra and numerical calculation.

In real life, the model must be a good deal more elaborate than it has been possible to show here, and there are a number of tools available which are more powerful than simple calculation; for example general purpose simulation lanuguages, and also packages designed specifically to simulate computer hardware and software performance. Any of these would permit a much more realistic model of the behaviour of disk and tape drives, for example, than that used in chapter 6. Even so, a model is always an approximation to the real thing. How can we determine whether it does reflect the actual behaviour of a real system, and how can we refine and improve it?

There are a number of important decisions which must be made in the design of the recovery procedures for which one may need some guidance from a model. Some examples are: the contents and organisation of the journals, the organisation of dumps, partitioning the database into sections for partial dumps, and selecting the frequency of dumps and checkpoints. These depend on information which may not be available, and for which one can only substitute informed guesses. One may have only the manufacturer's estimate for the relaibility of a new piece of hardware, and little idea of the incidence of errors in input data or the frequency of operator mistakes. One's first attempt at modelling the recovery procedures is not likely to be very accurate, therefore, nor are the decisions based on it.

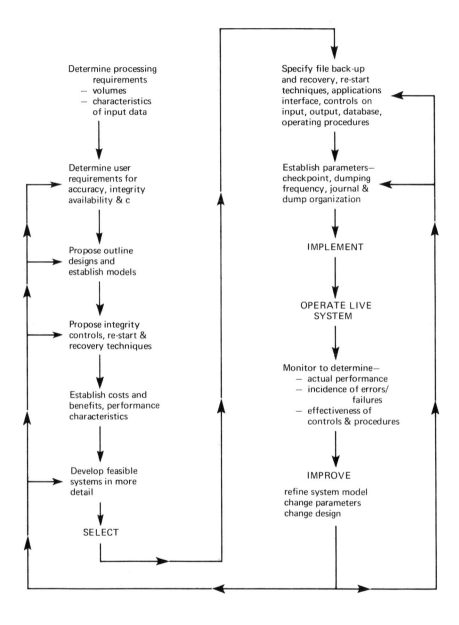

8.2   Integrity and recovery in system development

This means that one must build the model in the expectation that it will need to be modified and elaborated as new aspects of system behaviour come to light, and as more detailed information about its operating parameters becomes available. Even without full information, one can use the model to determine how sensitive the system is to the assumptions used. Equally, one should design the recovery system in such a way that the critical parameters can be readily changed.

Successive levels of refinement are based on statistics on the actual performance of development and live versions of the computer system. One needs detailed information on the frequency, extent, location and type of data errors and failures; the pattern of access to the database and the volume and distribution by type of transactions; the performance of each method of recovery, and the effect on system performance of logging, dumping and duplicate file updating – to name only a few examples. Only by collecting accurate statistics from the operational system can one discover whether the assumptions on which the design is based are valid.

So we come to the last stage of the process of "positive pessimism" described in the introduction. The designer has pursued with paranoiac determination the philosophy that whatever can go wrong, will go wrong, and he has built into his system facilities to detect and recover from every conceivable failure, however unlikely. On the day that his system goes live, if he has learnt his lesson well, he will already have resigned himself to the near certainty that he has forgotton something.

Table 8.1   System development - integrity and recovery considerations

Analysis and definition

Determine users' requirements for

- system availability, MTBF, MTTR
- fail-safety controls
- graceful degradation, fallback operation
- data accuracy and integrity
- performance: throughput, response times
- cost limitations

Determine processing requirements

- input transaction types, volumes, distribution in time
- file contents, sizes, access and update requirements and volumes
- quality of input data, likely error types and frequency

Determine reliability, performance, error-handling ability and cost of:

- hardware
- operating systems and other software packages
- programming languages

Propose outline solutions

- files and access methods, recovery techniques
- hardware configurations
- software, languages, packages
- build models of proposed solutions using
  - theoretical calculation
  - simulation languages
  - pilot schemes
- determine effect on overall performance and costs.

Design

Decide responsibility for

- input and output data validation
- integrity of stored data
- supervision of program and hardware errors
- transaction journal and audit trail management
- file recovery and program restart
- interface with operators

Design software structure and interfaces

- between supervisory programs and operating system
- amongst supervisory programs
- between supervisory programs and applications
  - for data management
  - for error handling
  - for recovery and restart

Determine file characteristies

- access method and organisation
- updating method
- record type and sizes, file sizes
- record linkages and pointers
- storage medium

Design recovery and backup for each file

- generation
- duplication

- dumping, incremental dumping
- audit trail

Design integrity controls

- input and output data validation
- checks on retrieved database records
- fail-safety checks
- deadlocks – detection, resolution, prevention
- checks on operators
- checks for correct versions of programs and files

Design fallback modes of operation

- reduced hardware configuration
- reduced terminal network
- partial loss of database
- partial program failures

Design restart/recovery database

- restart files – contents and protection
- dumps
    - organisation – logical or physical
    - database partitions for sectional dumps
    - physical storage, protection and control
- file generations
    - time cycles and retention periods
    - physical storage, protection and control
- audit trail and transaction journals
    - which to keep, and contents of each
    - organisation and storage medium
    - blocking, buffering, access methods
    - physical storage, protection and control
    - audit trail tag file applicable?
- checkpoint organization and contents

Design recovery procedures

- graded set of procedures according to failure
- scope of recovery
    - in time – single transaction/last checkpoint/last dump
    - single records/single files or sections/whole database
    - single program/groups of programs/whole system
- interface with application programs

- interface with terminal operators
- fault diagnosis and analysis procedures
- off-line file repair programs
- which procedures to use under what circumstances

Design statistics collection and analysis routines

Specify system tuning parameters

- placement on devices/units/channels of:
  - files and duplicates
  - journals, logs, tag files, etc
- dumping frequency
- checkpoint frequency

Refine model of chosen system

Implementation

Prepare comprehensive testing plans, including

- simulation and testing of failures
- failures during recovery

Impose strict controls on program quality, documentation, testing, acceptance

Provide documentation and training on recovery for:

- central operations staff
- terminal operators
- maintenance programmers

Use testing results to refine system model.

Operation

Collect and analyse statistics from:

- system monitoring output
- hardware logs
- operations records

On:

- hardware and software reliability
- location and type of program failures
- incidence of errors in input data and records retrieved from the database
- operators' mistakes or misunderstandings

Feed back to improve and enhance:

- hardware configuration
- hardware and software maintenance procedures
- software and applications programs
- documentation and training
- operational procedures
- system tuning parameters (dump, checkpoint frequency, etc)
- system model

Control changes to live programs, unscheduled changes to live data.

Index

V